Contents

DEDICATION

To my closest (You know who you are—**without you, I wouldn't be where I am and living such a Wellthy, Sovran life)**

and...

Humanity's youth—**your Sovranty matters, and best you figure that out sooner than later.**

This is a great place to start!

ACKNOWLEDGEMENTS

True resilience is not built in isolation. The very act of acknowledgment is a profound demonstration of the structural integrity at the heart of The Resiliency Code: honoring the interconnected systems that sustain us. This section represents more than gratitude; it is a mapping of the supportive architecture that made this work possible.

As we explore in these pages, collapse is optional only when we recognize and strengthen the connections that form our foundation. The people acknowledged here are not merely supporters; they are essential structural components in this manifestation of Sovran Wellth. Each played a role in maintaining integrity across the Nine Fields that comprise a resilient life.

The journey to create this book and operating system based on The Resiliency Code required pausing to honestly assess what was working and what wasn't, preparing through deep research and lived experience, and finally participating in the collaborative process of bringing these concepts to life.

What follows is a recognition of those who embodied these principles alongside me (or didn't), creating the capacity, jurisdiction, and contractual agreements that allowed The Resilient Path to emerge.

BY THE NINE FIELDS OF SOVRAN WELLTH

1. PHYSICAL: The Foundation of Capacity

To those who sustained the physical foundation that made this work possible:

Kim, whose unwavering presence provided the stability and strength that allowed me to build this operating system. Your commitment to creating environments of physical well-being, being emotionally rock-steady in my greatest times of need and your ever-present spiritual companionship created the space where these ideas could flourish.

Mom, Darrell and Karen: you provided me the unconditional love and support necessary for the physical creation of this work.

My closest colleagues at the AMA, ABN Amro Bank, Aon, Innovative, Meridian IT, Meridian Leasing, Information Technology Partners, Z Sphere and other entrepreneurial teams whose collaboration in developing physical systems and operational structures demonstrated what true resilience looks like in embodied form.

My friends who provided me a home-away-from-home during the many months of travel and time to curate this work in solitude.

2. EMOTIONAL: The Nervous System of Stability

To those who offered emotional regulation and stability during this journey:

Kim, the incarnation of a guardian angel in my life.

Nicole Connor, Resiliency Code co-creator, ecosystem brainchild, master strategist, book editor, book reviewer, and gifted designer. Your ability to collaborate in the navigation of complex landscapes while maintaining clarity and an ability to "stand fast" with field integrity exemplifies the resilient systems described in these pages.

Mom and Dad, whose emotional resilience throughout life's challenges has been a living example of what it means to maintain emotional Sovranty even in turbulent times.

3. INTELLECTUAL: The Framework of Sovran Thought

To those who contributed to the intellectual architecture of this work:

Nicole, Tom and Adam whose brilliant minds asked the necessary questions that refined these concepts into their most potent forms.

Those who engaged in countless hours of intellectual discourse, challenging assumptions and strengthening the framework's philosophical underpinnings.

4. CREATIVE: The Engine of Expansion

To those who fueled the creative expression of these concepts:

The design team at Sovran Press, particularly Nicole Connor, who transformed abstract concepts into visual language that speaks directly to the reader's creative capacity.

MRS (My Resilient Self).

The Z Sphere team and collaborators, whose support and commitment throughout the last decade embodies the creative expansion this work promotes.

5. CONNECTION: The Stability of Right Relationship

To those who maintained right relationship throughout this process:

The early readers and community members who provided feedback and formed the first circle of connection around these ideas. Your willingness to engage deeply with this material strengthened the field that supports it.

The broader Resilient Path community, whose genuine connections demonstrate how these principles create networks of support rather than dependence.

6. VOCATION: The System of Self-Sustenance

To those whose vocational alignment made this project sustainable:

Our publishing partners, whose commitment to their craft ensured this message would reach those who need it most.

Mentors and guides such as Kim, Darrell, Tom, Don B., Lou N., Paul, Lou C., Charlie D., Charlie S., Charles A., Ray C., Bert, Adam M., H, Paul, Mike W., Jim C., Chad and RJ, who helped shape my vocational path toward becoming a living example of this work rather than merely its creator.

7. ENVIRONMENT: The Structure of Space

To those who created environments where this work could thrive:

Kim, Tom, Dave, Kory, Shawna, Al, Jim M., Mike S., Ray C., Ray Jr., Bobby and Jamey, whose support and care for our physical environment provided the inspirational space where much of this writing took place.

Those who provided necessary experiences in failure to foster even greater levels of resiliency: Bill, Ken, Dorie, Barry, Ray O., Adam D., Phil N., Bob N., Erik, Kory, Joe B., Pier, John, Ben, Peter C., and Javier.

Those who maintain our digital environments, creating spaces where these ideas can be shared globally without losing their integrity.

8. RESOURCES: The Channels of Flow

To those who ensured resources flowed appropriately throughout this project:

Our financial supporters and early backers, who recognized the value of this work and ensured it had the necessary resources to reach completion.

The resource coordinators who managed the practical aspects of bringing a book from concept to reality, maintaining integrity in every transaction.

9. FAITH: The Anchor of Meaning

To those who helped maintain faith in this mission:

The ancestors and wisdom keepers whose teachings informed the spiritual underpinnings of this framework.

You, the reader, whose faith in possibility brought you to these pages and whose implementation of these principles will prove that collapse truly is optional when we align with the natural laws of resilience.

In acknowledging each of you through the lens of the Nine Fields, I demonstrate not just gratitude but recognition of how true resilience emerges from structural integrity across all domains of life. This book exists because each of you maintained your Sovran Wellth in ways that supported mine.

With profound appreciation and in service to our collective resilience,

— David Atkinson

HYPERLINKS REFERENCE

N EARLY 200 HYPERLINKS are provided in this work: valuable resources to reference and/or acquire in building your personal resiliency.

Throughout the book, you'll see words with a (*) next to them: these have a hyperlink in this supplement.

Scan this code to access your hyperlinks supplement:

What you'll get:

- All web resources referenced throughout the book with clickable links for immediate access

- Larger pictures of the images in the book

- Updated resources as they become available

ACCESS INSTRUCTIONS BELOW

Instructions:

1. Open your phone's camera app

2. Point camera at the QR code

3. Tap the notification that appears

4. Enter the password found in the "About the Author" section to access your supplement document

5. Enjoy the adventure!

Bookmark this page: you may want to reference these resources multiple times as you apply The Resiliency Code principles and walk THE RESILIENT PATH.

00 - SIGNAL CREATES STRUCTURE: A CYMATIC PROLOGUE

S everal years ago, I discovered the power of Cymatics*: the effect of sound on physical matter. The image below is generated with sound.

Yes, that's a thing...the words (sound) that come out of your mouth have power! Try this little experiment to see what I mean. Right now, speak the words to yourself out loud: *I am somebody*. Yes, I know...feels weird and silly, but do it. Say it again. How did that feel? Did it feel good? A wise, highly successful, German-American mentor of mine taught me this simple thing several decades ago, one of many experiences that started me on my path to personal resilience.

We've all known deep down since we were born that words make a difference, but it often takes us until later in life to "re-learn" and appreciate what that means. Its why certain music resonates well with each of us individually. Each song has a harmony that aligns well with our physical, electrically-charged bodies! I'm confident the Founding Fathers of the US knew about the power of sound and words, which is why I believe the First Amendment to the US Constitution is the First. They knew: the words have power, *which is why they are so clearly remembered as powerful speakers, writers, and orators in general.*

Free speech is a necessity for free men. The quotes from Jefferson, Franklin, Washington, Jackson, Madison, and on and on. Awe inspiring stuff. Clearly, they were serious. I mean, if the words didn't work, well, then, there's the 2nd Amendment to back up the 1st! Let's look to another example: The KJV (King James Version) Bible. What does it say?

John 1:1 "In the beginning was the Word, and the Word was with God, and the Word was God." Last time I checked, it doesn't get any bigger than the bible and other ancient religious texts such as the Tanakh, Vedas, Buddhist Canons, and countless others. Point is, regardless of your beliefs, cymatics is a real phenomenon at the very center of human existence and experience.

The words, language and interpretations literally matter—*they are the signals that create the structures of your reality.* You might be saying to yourself, why should I care? Because the world is changing rapidly, and *rapid change creates unprecedented opportunities to build structures that persist for generations.* The old structures are failing, which means the field is wide open for those who understand how signals create lasting architecture. In order to build generational resilience, we must stop, look and listen: to recognize the signals around us, see clearly what structures are collapsing versus what's emerging, then take the necessary steps to align our signals with the structures that *maximize human potential*.

What I didn't fully understand until recent years was that every experience documented in these pages (from the financial collapse that forced me to rebuild from nothing, to the relationship failures that taught me where I was abandoning myself, to the moments of standing alone when everyone else folded) was teaching me to develop what most people seek externally through ASMR videos: autonomous nervous system regulation. While millions search for temporary calm through whispered voices and tapping sounds, I was unknowingly developing permanent structural sovereignty. Each crisis became a masterclass in reading my body's native intelligence before breakdown hit. Each pressure point taught me to pause, prepare, and participate from unshakable internal authority rather than reactive chaos. This isn't about enduring stress: it's about building a nervous system so structurally sound that what breaks others only reveals your true capacity. The difference between external regulation and internal mastery is the difference between borrowing calm and owning it. Working with Nicole Connor, we've distilled these field-tested methods into both the strategic AI partner you'll meet (My Resilient Self) and The Field Guide curriculum that teaches you to become your own source of regulation. What took me decades of trial by fire, you can learn systematically in a highly condensed time frame. Because when your nervous system becomes your trusted ally instead of your greatest liability, collapse becomes optional, and that changes everything.

This simple process is called: **Pause. Prepare. Participate.** I've been unknowingly using this process and its underlying "code" for many decades. It's called *The Resiliency Code*. The experiences in this book are a direct reflection of using this process on my life's journey down The Resilient Path. This is the first book in THE RESILIENT PATH series, and I titled it "COLLAPSE:

IT'S OPTIONAL" because that's exactly what I discovered—each crisis, each near-death experience, each moment of having to rebuild proved that collapse wasn't inevitable when proper structure exists. Like metal shaped by fire and hammer, my capacity to navigate life's challenges has been forged into something unshakable, demonstrating that collapse truly is optional when you understand how *signals create lasting structure.*

The ecosystem on the Sovran Systems Institute website* provides you with a systematic path to Sovran Wellth. You'll work through a structured process built upon The Resiliency Code that brings clarity to your life's misalignments, helping you identify and eliminate blind spots before they derail your progress. When issues surface, they become valuable lessons—small, fast failures that strengthen your foundation rather than stopping your momentum.

This systematic approach develops your ability to see with such clarity that you maximize value from every interaction and experience. You'll spot opportunities others miss and navigate trouble with precision, much like I do in my capacity as a licensed USCG Master Captain navigating one of the most hazardous bodies of water* in the world.

The tangible outcome of this systematic approach is Sovran Wellth*—not just financial prosperity, but **structural integrity across all dimensions of your life.**

Here's where it gets exponential. When you intentionally use this approach, you don't just create value for yourself, you also provide value to others. Have you created any YouTube videos lately on how to repair a car or on how to make a cool and unique gift for someone? How to get better results from AI interactions?

Your cycle of research, practice, reflect and refine becomes valuable guidance for the next person building comprehensive resilience.

Here's the key difference: *Content or "value" creators chase external validation and revenue streams.* **Sovran Wellth builders create internal alignment that draws sustainable prosperity to them.**

I've experienced life-changing situations ranging from the worst of the worst to the best of the best! A person is not able to pilot an ice-breaking vessel on Lake Michigan in late January through 2 FEET of solid ice, recover hundreds of millions of dollars of lost financial transaction data for a Fortune 100 investment bank or create the world's first fully sustainable and disaster resilient building system* *unless they have Sovran Wellth.*

Yes, that's me, no B.S. The proof is in the results.

Used a 14" bar chainsaw to cut into 2+ feet of ice to help break the 50' steel icebreaker loose and take divers out for an emergency dive inspection required on a utility fresh water intake pipe.

Now I'm going to show you exactly how I built that capability and how you can build yours. The experiences that follow in this book demonstrate The Resiliency

Code in action across real-world challenges—from cutting into 2+ feet of ice with a chainsaw to break a 50' steel icebreaker loose, to navigating financial collapse, to creating sustainable solutions for communities.

Each example reveals specific methods and resources you can use to build Sovran Wellth that *creates lasting value for generations.*

Let's begin.

In our modern world, remember this. All things considered; our quality of life depends on our access to energy. Access to clean water, access to food, access to fuel, access to transportation are a few examples at the top of that list, because they all depend on energy;

• to pump and filter the water

• to grow, harvest and process the food

• to extract, refine and distribute the fuel

• to manufacture, distribute, sell and maintain cars, trucks, trains and ships

Credit to Lawrence Livermore National Laboratory* for the chart below; they've been doing detailed analysis and statistics on US Energy production and consumption for decades. They are one of the few "go-to" authorities on the subject. A hat tip also to Dr. Chris Martenson of www.peakprosperity.com* for bringing my attention to this highly valuable data! The following chart is just one example from decades of experience and several thousand data points which I've personally used to validate the solutions and recommendations in the chapters that follow:

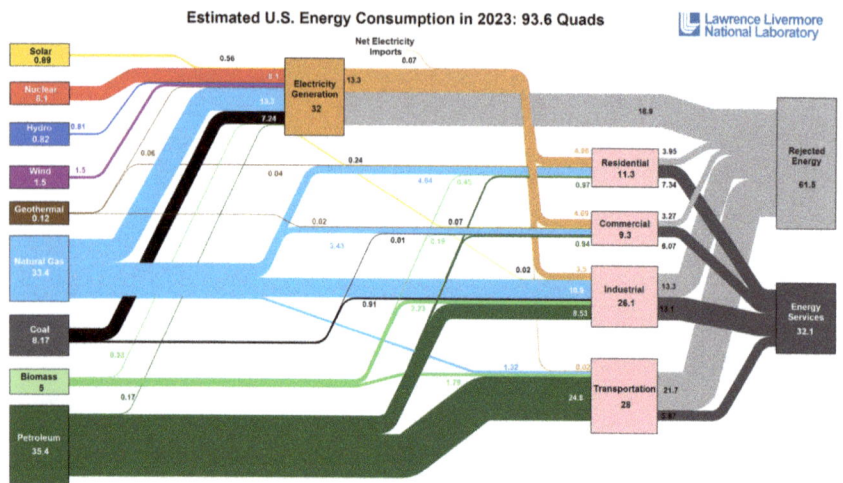

Here's two specific things to notice from the Energy Consumption chart above:

1) Solar and wind power generation account for approximately 2.6% of US energy production. (0.89+1.5/93.4) = 2.6%. Is that what you were expecting?

2) The little orange line from the "Electricity Generation" section which connects to the "Transportation" section shows an amount of .02 "Quads" of electricity used for transportation (28) which is equal to .0007 (effectively zero).

What does this mean? First, it means that as of 2023 and after spending a few decades of time, hundreds of thousand acres of farmland and billions in subsidies for residential solar installations, commercial solar installations, and commercial wind farms, we've hardly begun to scratch the surface of moving away from petroleum energy sources!

Second, it means that as of 2023 with billions in subsidies for electric cars, buses, and other commercial transportation projects, *effectively zero percent* of US annual transportation needs are powered purely by electricity!

I hate to be the bearer of bad news, but investments to date in solar power, wind power, and electric cars are not even close to helping transition our energy production and transportation to non-petroleum alternatives, which means they weren't "investments" at all. *It was something else*, which I leave up to you to figure out, keeping in mind, the most obvious answer is probably the right one. Think of all the energy, water, oil, balsa wood*, fiberglass, minerals, copper, silver, steel, concrete and human effort that went into the "green" infrastructures you see across the country today. It's a mind-boggling amount when you think about it! These are just two data points from thousands which support this short and comprehensive book.

I'm all about seeking alternatives that make sense environmentally, economically, and socially, but Western culture's expectations must change of "electric everything" being a solution to our energy needs. The way it's been implemented around the world today is not viable as a long-term solution, and certainly not to the general public in developed nations. Are electric-powered vehicles useless? No, they definitely have a viable place in our future for specific applications.

Where's your blind spot?

The above data points and perspective have shown me that surviving and thriving in the future in large part depends on preserving America's remaining strength, stability and integrity, regardless of where you are in the world. Utilizing all that America still has to offer and quickly learning, knowing, and using at least a few of the simple secrets to creating a resilient life in the chapters that follow is going to matter—big time. This applies to everyone, poor, rich or in-between, and regardless of who is our President. It also doesn't hurt to have a little luck, faith, focus and to do some work! When the credit bubble of the late 1920s burst, every American was instantly thrown into turmoil. Massive fortunes were lost and made, and innovation, frugality, and resourcefulness flourished. *All structural indicators point to another such period unfolding* **right now.**

During the early 1930s, even the smallest visionaries thrived and were able to create massive wealth spanning generations, if they had "tangible resources" and knew how to collaborate well with others! I'm an American, so there's a bias towards my American lens and experience in the chapters that follow, however, I've traveled the world and have a profound respect for all cultures and perspectives. I've yet to find a modern, comprehensive guide which specifically recommends what the "tangible resources" are and how to collaborate with others!

This book is just that.

It's taken me more than 40 years to accumulate and distill the information and experiences in the chapters that follow. Most of the pieces of the puzzle are scattered throughout several thousand books, podcasts, live events, and internet interviews from different people. What you won't find anywhere is a real-world operational system which brings all of these pieces and personal experience together. Decades of trial and error have shown which of these experiences work best in the real-world!

After reading this book and learning about the personal resiliency ecosystem myself and Nicole Connor have created, you can be confident you'll be way ahead of the curve and be in a position to contribute to the resiliency of communities in the coming years by collaborating with your family, friends, neighbors, and fellow countrymen to not just survive, but to thrive! On your journey to achieving a sustainable and resilient life in modern times, you must learn the value of patience, simplicity and development of good habits, all essential to: **Pause. Prepare. Participate.**

Fast, uninformed, knee-jerk-emotional decisions when it comes to your health, shelter, water, food, communications, relationships, employment, finances, transportation, and political engagements in the years ahead will likely lead to a life of confusion, catastrophe and possibly the end of your mortality (or someone else's). Yes, it's that serious and one of several reasons why wars and conflict start. *The "Polycrisis" is here.* The common question I've most recently been asked by dozens of family, friends, and professional colleagues is "What do I do?" Well...treat this book as a great starting point to be your guide as you begin your journey down The Resilient Path.

My life experiences on the journey to "Be Resilient" have included countless disappointments, betrayals, lost loved-ones, financial reset (to zero), physical suffering, personal burnout, professional burnout, humility, enlightenment, camaraderie, true love, major breakthroughs, financial frugality and the development of an acute sense of self-awareness. The following chapters are a distillation of those experiences to put forth the ultimate "guide" of where to start, what to do and in what place you should ultimately be. Worrying and obsessing about things outside of your control are wasted energy! I encourage you to do ONE small thing every day to accomplish a task towards improving your personal resiliency...a month or two from now, you'll be amazed at what you've accomplished!

Bold text and grey callout boxes highlight important guidance throughout the book. Substack readers can click links directly. Print and e-book readers: phrases or words marked with (*) are links to valuable information in the separate hyperlink reference, accessible by scanning the QR code at the beginning or end of the book. I cannot emphasize enough the need to focus on building a simple, stable foundation of basic essentials that provide confidence through good or bad experiences in which you grow and maintain momentum. *Everyone's journey is their own.* The real secret is to test your simple preparations and use well-informed decision-making on a consistent, regular basis, to get comfortable with your life skills and preparedness resources and use them in a collaborative way with others not just to survive, but to thrive in spite of the looming hardships!

Keep in mind, if you live in the city, you are vulnerable to disruption. While much of this guide can be applied to city life, rural communities are the place to be and will provide the greatest opportunity to thrive! How many times do we have to witness people being wiped out in America and around the world by a hurricane, flood, tornado, fire, earthquake or man-made disaster before we change our ways? It's not because you don't want to or don't have the ability to. Geographical vulnerability is only part of the structural problem.

For instance, in America, we've allowed this to happen; Thomas Jefferson wrote: *"I believe that banking institutions are more dangerous to our liberties than standing armies. If the American people ever allow private banks to control the issue of their currency, first by inflation, then by deflation, the banks and corporations that will grow up around (these banks) will deprive the people of all property until their children wake up homeless on the continent their fathers conquered."* My fellow Americans, what do you see happening around you today? Exactly what Thomas Jefferson predicted above, because he and the other Founding Fathers had seen it before!

I'm grateful for all the courageous men, women and children in America and around the world who've taken action and even paid the ultimate sacrifice to support people in times of need and impossible circumstances. Cowards and liars with bad intentions beware...

It's not going to be smooth sailing for everyone. There are many issues to work through as Americans and humanity in general, however, the steps you take in this book to improve your personal resiliency will determine how much or how little you are affected by the significant changes coming. *Nothing external to you is going to save you*—no politicians, no celebrities, no business moguls, no alt-media personalities, just you and your natural ability to work effectively with others. The viable path forward is possible by utilizing the resources Nicole Connor and I have created: to achieve clarity, build confidence and develop skills to navigate it. It's clear to me and by now should be clear to you that there's no organized entity of any kind that has, or is willing to, move the needle to fix the problems! I know this because I've studied the problems and worked diligently for the last 20 years *finding solutions that do fix the problems.*

I can say with 100% confidence that with a fraction of the resources as modern approaches waste every day, it is possible to fix the biggest problems we face as a global humanity. *We have a resource allocation problem, not a resource availability problem.* It takes courage and responsibility as individuals, coupled with benevolent leadership, to assist humanity in correcting these problems. Characteristics sorely lacking in the world today! The Resilient Path to sustainable and resilient living is not only possible, but required in order for all of humanity to move forward.

If we don't, we risk taking a huge leap backwards when the global systems we've come to rely on catastrophically break, which is where many of us know we're going if something doesn't change and change very soon. You've probably noticed by now that in spite of the massive generosity of individuals, corporations, celebrities, non-profits, etc. and hundreds of billions in donations, nothing has changed. It's because the current way we're doing things isn't sustainable and will not fix the problems we face. That's the narrative trap of the Victim, Villain, Hero loop*.

The evidence speaks for itself. Thousands of experts and thousands of organizations worldwide have wielded hundreds of billions in funding to tackle these problems for decades, yet here we are, experiencing the same crises that plagued us 50+ years ago. Why? Because we're trapped in this loop. A loop that mistakes symptoms for causes, and temporary fixes for permanent, structural solutions.

I know because I've read tens of thousands of papers, posts, books, listened to the experts, read the project proposals, read the grant award lists, met with the GOs, and worked with several non-profits. Being an American and having witnessed the systematic exploitation of our country during the course of my life thus far, we must bring America back to a position of a strong middle class, smaller government, leading by example through peaceful, constructive outcomes, and once again become the admiration of the world. The relative peace we've experienced around the world in recent decades is the exception, not the rule. Centuries of evidence support the fact that in the absence of strong leadership, healthy trade, good communication between nations, and a vibrant, confident, working class, the world can be a very ugly, painful and cruel place.

Make yourself comfortable, grab something to drink, enjoy the book and have fun learning from the experiences and resources that follow, on your journey to be personally resilient. After all, making the world a better place happens one person at a time!

01 - WHAT HAPPENED TO THE AMERICA WE KNEW AND HOW TO GET IT BACK!

I'm a middle-class American of Scottish-English-Native American descent, born in a Midwestern town in the late 1960s, an era where honesty, trust, and virtue were a norm. It wasn't perfect, but life was generally good. EVERY town had a hardware store, a drugstore, gas station, and restaurant.

Everyone in town knew the owners and understood the importance of the services and goods those businesses brought to the local community. Small regional radio stations were commonplace. Long-standing manufacturing businesses and household names such as Allis-Chalmers in SE Wisconsin employed tens of thousands of Americans, and were beacons of innovation, powering American farms and industrial equipment. Public utilities such as Commonwealth Edison (a regulated monopoly) and manufacturers like Allis-Chalmers were the pillars of American greatness.

Across America, starting in the late 70s/early 80s, companies like Allis-Chalmers were slowly replaced by just a few large, private corporations through corruption, political lobbying, massive regional-then-national consolidation, de-regulation, off-shoring and other slow-moving, erosive currents. For me and the rest of the American population, those currents have resulted in a hyper-consolidation of wealth in fewer hands, ecological destruction, two-tier legal system, widespread addiction to technology/substance-abuse/pornography, continuous loss of dollar purchasing power, depletion of nutrients in food, intense urbanization, electricity monopolies, commodity-education, out-of-control property tax bills, and media monopolies. What we have witnessed is a slow-motion collapse of our rural communities and private small businesses which has resulted in a fragile, on-edge, potentially perilous situation for the average American quality of life. Most don't even know it, some don't care and the few that do care, don't really know how to fix it.

I was blessed and am grateful to have had highly respected parents in our community when I was growing up. They set an outstanding example for me to follow. They supported and guided me through all the ups and downs of my life. Although I made so many mistakes, I learned, was taught, and know how to win! I'm grateful to have experienced being:

- an exceptional high-honor-roll student

- a tall, good-looking, but foolish young man who made MANY mistakes

- an extremely gifted, natural athlete. In 1987, at 18 years of age, 6'5" and 235 lbs., I consistently ran a 4.5-4.6 second 40-yard dash*! (Rare at that time for a young man of my size)

- a high-school Academic All American (thank you for the nomination, Richard Hyde*, may you RIP)

- a championship baseball player scouted for 10 years by several MLB teams and drafted* in the 43rd round by the Toronto Blue Jays at the age of 18

- a devoted husband (I unfortunately failed the first time)

- a good father, but like most made many mistakes, but always had and will have the best intentions

- an Information Technology Systems Engineer and Architect for 30-years, innovating with some of the world's largest, most advanced, state-of-the-art technology providers like Sun Microsystems, EMC, Oracle, Netapp, StorageTek, MTI, OpenVision/Veritas, Commvault, Citrix, Netware, Nutanix, HP, IBM, Sybase, Informix, SuperMicro, Onshape, Autodesk, Solidworks, PTC, Clearcase and Xyvision.

- a manager of multi-million-dollar, audited budgets

- a second-generation business operator of a 54-year-old business (thank you Mom, Dad and our clients)

- a visionary entrepreneur

- gifted with the ability to see trends of things to come 8-10 years in advance (until recently, it's been more of a curse than a blessing!)

- a close collaborator with more than a dozen of the top global minds in their areas of expertise: Oracle's Ecosystem, Highly Available Computer Systems with Zero Downtime, Diesel Engines, Utility Scale Power Generation/Distribution, State-of-the-art Stock Trading Systems & Algorithms, Fisheries Ecosystem Biology, Maritime Navigation & Operations, Construction (Bridges, Skyscrapers, Power Plant), Water Treatment Methods, Holistic Wellness, Dentistry, etc.

I've applied this winning (and losing) experience to being a tenacious entrepreneur who's determined to change the world for the better. I've also figured out the unique value of major failure and total loss. Speaking of experience, here's an example of my father's unique mentoring style, in the early 1980s, on a crisp, cold, raw, January winter day with 10-15' waves, 32 miles out in the middle of Lake Michigan (think Deadliest Catch*)—out of the blue, while pulling up nets, my father looked at me and asked me the most peculiar question: *"son, do you know what the best experience is?"* As a young teenage boy going through puberty, I'm thinking to myself my father is going to give me some invaluable advice about dating or the birds and the bees. He waited and watched me contemplate a possible answer, any answer, to this strange question, and after about 10 seconds when I didn't respond, he answered it for me: **bad experience**. The cliffhanger of all cliffhanger questions from a father to his teenage son and all I got was "bad experience?" It left an impression on me, so much so, to this day I vividly remember his face as he told me those words, and how I felt. Little did I realize how right he was and how much I've come to appreciate his words of wisdom that day. Knowing what I know, he was not only right, *he was so right*.

Good experience is great, but bad experience is invaluable—**it's what teaches us emotionally-charged life lessons that make us who we are!** It's also why we so vividly remember very specific childhood experiences. Be sure to store what you just read in your memory. *In a future chapter, I discuss the importance of epigenetics and The Resiliency Code in building Sovran Wellth.* Being over 50 years old, I've witnessed how many people keep repeating the same life experience over and over again until in an instant they "realize" and "decide" that they must do something different to improve their situation! The life lesson I learned from these observations was how to fail fast and small, minimizing the disruption to my life and degradation of my health. To top it all off, I learned in my early 40's the real value of human mortality and how precious life and our time on earth is. I experienced several life-altering events in the span of two short years:

- Finalized a multi-year, brutal divorce after 17 years of marriage

- A catastrophic truck wreck

- A near miss by inches from a falling 70' Sweetgum tree

- I survived brain cancer after the removal of a stage 4 golf ball-sized brain tumor attached to my brain stem.

These two years felt like an eternity! Pictures are worth 1000 words:

Never saw it coming. Reckless driver pit-maneuvered my truck at highway speed. I walked away and kept building without missing a beat. This is what structural preparedness looks like. Collapse is optional when the foundation holds.

I was standing here

Heard a small crack like dry wood breaking. In that split second, I saw the massive tree falling toward me and made it to safety with giant strides. Had I been on my phone or listening to music, I'd have been crushed. Situational awareness isn't optional, it's survival architecture.

ACOUSTIC NEUROMA
(VESTIBULAR SCHWANNOMA)

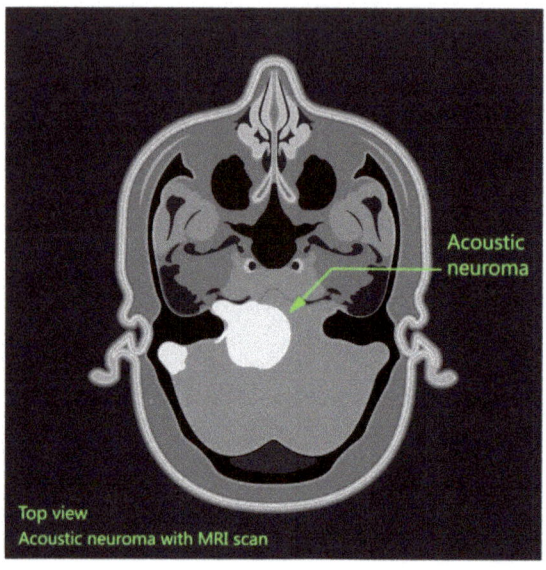

Top view
Acoustic neuroma with MRI scan

First surgeon I was referred to (one of the "best" in the country) triggered my internal alarm twice: 'RUN AWAY FROM THIS DOCTOR.' I paused instead of reacting. Following that inner guidance led me to the right surgeon with 98% success rate. Structural integrity creates space to receive life-saving messages. Trust your internal compass. It reads what external authority misses.

Image credit:

https://avcphysio.com.au/service/vestibular-schwannoma-acoustic-neuroma (sample image, my original was unavailable)

I am blessed to have an angel on my shoulder. I survived the multi-year, chronic, high-intensity stress of the divorce and destruction of relationships with my children, I walked away with a small scratch from the car wreck, escaped within inches of being crushed by the tree and made nearly a 100% recovery from the brain surgery. Unfortunately, the brain surgery was a rough ride. The surgery induced 24x7 vertigo for 6 months, required I re-learn how to walk, re-learn how to speak, re-learn how to type and re-learn how to hear the location of voices and noises (I temporarily lost my "stereo" hearing). This was all due to the required disruption of my hearing, balance and facial nerves to perform the surgery. After the vertigo subsided, I made an exceptionally quick recovery over several months in spite of all the "odds" due to much of what I share in this book.

I understand adversity, tenacity, recovery and resiliency! If you think for a second, I survived this alone, you're sorely mistaken. The value of a devoted spouse, family, friends, community and collaboration to my recovery and the path to a resilient life will become clear in later chapters. Somewhere along the way, I figured out two of the mandatory requirements for getting America back to where it used to be: personal resiliency and personal responsibility.

This book and other works in the Resilient Path series provide a frame of reference from personal experiences and use of The Resiliency Code, demonstrating why these two key personal attributes above are required to travel The Resilient Path. I've observed how incredibly fragile we as Americans have become. Whether it's emotions, mental health, physical health, bad decisions, rabbit-holes of assumptions, poor communication, unhealthy relationships, leveraged finances, toxic work environment, food/drug/porn/gaming/social media addictions, living conditions or vehicle driving habits, there's typically several issues facing all of us at any given time.

For instance, have you ever seen what happens when the power goes out at a store and it will only accept cash instead of cards? It's incredible. People complain and/or walk out since 60-70% nowadays pay with a card of some sort. People who are used to paying with cash don't miss a beat! I also figured out that we have voluntarily been convinced or duped to abdicate* or subrogate* most of the essential responsibilities in our lives! Attorneys, Investment Brokers, Accountants, School Boards, Teachers, Doctors, Mechanics, and HOAs are just a few examples...

Having come to this realization, and after more than a decade of searching, I could not find a comprehensive, well-researched, practical, action-oriented mentorship program, community group, system or framework for re-empowering myself and others in such a way where we could collaborate and quickly revitalize American rural communities. Given the size of the task and fact that an effective path did not exist, after much personal reflection and discussion with family, close friends, and dozens of professional colleagues, myself and co-creator Nicole Connor decided to develop one. This is how to get America back to what it was (and better)—**but it will require commitment, resources, leadership and action to restore American resiliency!**

At the core of what we've created is The Resiliency Code: a literal operating system for building unshakable individual resilience in the form of Sovran Wellth. Typical outcomes include:

- pre-empting obstacles by seeing them with clarity

- achieving sustainable momentum (not burning out and starting over)

- transformation without crisis (moving out of the intentional destruction and re-build model in place today)

A revitalization can happen, one person at a time, each at their own pace and way! Throughout this book you'll find my personal experiences which reveal the simple, small steps to take now to be one of these people and contribute to an American Renaissance that lasts for generations. Step out of the Victim, Villain, Hero loop, utilize The Resiliency Code and create your own Resilient Path. Go to the Sovran Systems Institute website* to begin your personal journey to *be resilient.*

02 - WHEN THEY COME THIRSTY: PREPARING FOR THE WATER CRISIS NO ONE WANTS TO DISCUSS

One of my favorite movies is "Sahara" with Humphrey Bogart: it's a WWII movie set in the N. African desert about a very small rag-tag group of Allied soldiers seeking a safe path to escape from a rapidly advancing German Army.

The problem they face is that it's a harsh desert, far from resupply and there's no water to be found anywhere. Sgt. Joe Gunn (Bogart) and his group manage to escape but are quickly discovered by a large unit of the German Army at a dry well they attempted to get water from.

The unit pursuing them is out of water and Sgt. Gunn comes up with an ingenious strategy to hold out long enough in the hopes that reinforcements will arrive in time. The end is genuinely suspenseful and has many surprises! Believing there was water at the well, the desperate German Army screams for Wasser! and reveals the true value of water and makes it clear why it's your #1 priority (Wasser is the German word for water). If you'd like to watch the movie, you can watch it here*.

I'm blessed to live in a rural community and have a large network of family, friends, neighbors and business colleagues. My greatest concern is that when the systems Americans have come to depend on do finally break, several dozen people will show up my door and be completely unprepared. I've had the opportunity to discuss America's devolving situation at great length with my network over the years, this one statement was made several times: "If something happens, I'll just come to your place." This one statement is in large part the inspiration for my efforts. How could so many of my fellow "resourceful" Americans be so unprepared? After all, that's part of what being an American is! The fact of the matter is that those that made that statement have forgotten the significance of this American trait and importance of it!

Should this ever happen to you (where people show up with nothing, expecting you to "take care of them"), respectfully give them a small amount of water and food and send them on their way. A difficult, uncomfortable decision? Yes. Must you do it? Absolutely, because if you are unprepared and unrealistic, deciding to take them in without the proper resources is a recipe for disaster. But, but, David, you must be compassionate...after all, God or the angels will save us!

Hogwash.

Empathetic. *I am.*

Know there is A Most High? *I do.*

I am also painfully aware of several examples throughout history where a group of people "left it up to God and the angels" to save them from being slaughtered, raped or sold into slavery when the enemy was at the gates. Yep, it's happened many, many times in history. An example of this I recently discovered comes from my reading of the book "The End of Everything*" by Victor Davis Hanson. It's well-written and definitely worth the time to read or listen to the audiobook. Many Constantinople residents during the last days of the fall of the city in 1453 believed an angel would descend from heaven to save them at the last moment—**it didn't happen**. They were slaughtered, profusely raped, sold into slavery or lucky enough to be one of a few who escaped. This may sound harsh (and it is), but the bottom-line is that I discovered how imperative it is to be realistic about people, circumstances, resources, and faith. **Hope is not a strategy, being resilient is**.

Start with the most important thing to human life besides air to breathe: *Water*. Water is essential for life and this one simple preparation can turbocharge your basic resiliency in a short period of time! Do not underestimate the importance of it and why it's imperative to first make sure enough clean drinking water is going to be available for you and those that depend on you, wherever you are! I also know that anyone thinking bottled water is going to solve this problem is dead wrong.

Besides being generally unhealthy when consumed in volume, when the bottled water quickly runs out in a crisis situation, it's one of the fastest ways to dehydration, dysentery* and death! I found the BEST thing to do personally, for family, a friend or even a stranger is to provide them the ability to filter their own drinking water and show them how to properly use it, like "teaching a man to fish" vs. giving a man a fish. This is the first and key step of just a few steps to achieve basic resiliency! When the time comes (and it will in my lifetime), a person's greatest value will be their wit, knowledge, practical skills and access to resources.

My go-to choices to be resilient when it comes to potable water are: Berkey, Dry Element and Sawyer. Pay attention to the details below, they will make or break your experience with each of the systems. When discretionary funds are available, acquire TRAVEL/PERSONAL FILTER(S). Keep a travel/personal filter in your purse, backpack, computer bag or travel suitcase at all times (I recommend the cost-effective 4-pack*). Use Sawyer Mini's for personal needs and family dependents. When dry, there are zero issues bringing these through airport security screening, except maybe as a conversation starter!

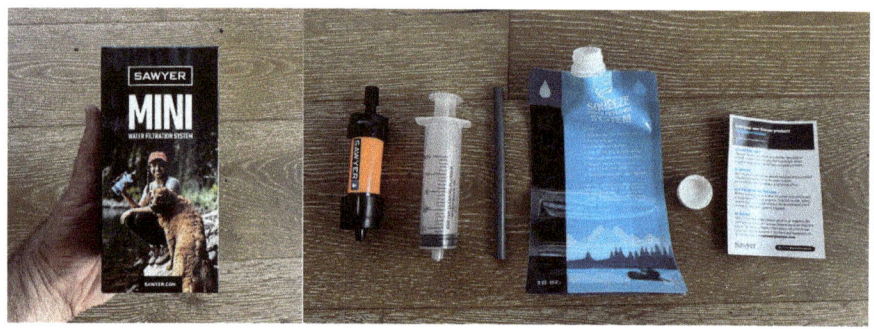

RESILIENT PATH INSIGHT: You'll find one of the most important things you must do after using a Sawyer Mini with dirty or sediment-filled-water is, when possible and practical, to back flush it thoroughly not long after you use it (when the filter element is still wet). Filtering clear rainwater or clean stream water are less of an issue. Back-flushing greatly extends the useful life of the filter and results and greater resiliency when adversity strikes!

Gravity Water Filter

Next, acquire a gravity water filter for each family household. There are many quality manufacturers out there like Dry Element*, Berkey, Aquacera, Propur or Doulton.

My 10+ year "Big Berkey:" 2.25-gallon stainless steel, excellent performance/looks. Recent Dry Element filter upgrade: works like a charm!

They're super easy to use and keep clean. For example, buy one Nano Gravity Water Purification System from Dry Element, one or more spare filters and **be sure to buy a spare dispensing spigot**! When the spigot breaks off while moving the system at some point and there's not a spare, the reason for the suggestion will be obvious! Already own a Berkey, Aquacera, Propur or Doulton system? GREAT: buy the Dry Element Nano Filter cartridges as backups or to use instead of the ceramic or other filters the systems came with.

BE RESILIENT TIP: Berkey system owners, especially owners of the PF-2 Fluoride removal filters: take care to not over-tighten them, or just don't risk using them. There's well-documented evidence that if overtightened, damage to the filter media can occur, discharging unsafe levels of Aluminum into the filtered drinking water! Myself and others recently became aware that the makers of the Berkey system are involved in multiple lawsuits pertaining to their filter methods and components, so do your own diligence! FWIW, in my experience, they make a solid product in terms of the containers: high quality, look great, easy to clean and easy to use!

Lawsuit Statement*

Berkey Suit Against EPA*

The reality is, SERIOUS homesteaders have preparations for a handful of people and several months of water at most. It's just simple math, time and reality. Most "talk the talk," but very few actually have the resources to "walk the walk." My experience has shown that about 3 people out of 100 take action on their own or based on recommendations I've made. If you're reading this, you are likely to be one of the three who have or will! I'll buy gifts for family and friends during holidays or for birthdays which consist of water filtration solutions for times of need! Sounds corny...but not for long! In the near future, it will be a blessing for someone to have practical knowledge and experience with personal water filtration devices or gravity-fed, household-scale drinking water systems for immediate family and closest friends. What a conversation piece for future generations when it comes time to use it! Remember when uncle David bought us the water filters? It was a life saver!

Bulk Water Storage

Here's an example of one 1,550-gallon tank I've installed: full and ready when needed!

If discretionary funds and space are available: Acquire a tank* to store a large volume of water. Pick a place near a residence or just outside a secure building, level the ground, place and fill the BLACK or GREEN plastic potable water storage tank on the ground that's been leveled. Prior to filling, install a hose bib at the top (for filling) and hose bib at the bottom (for dispensing) and get a 50' RV water hose*. Always have a spare hose! The dark plastic tank keeps your water protected from sunlight/algae growth, contamination or theft and the hose bibs make it easy to fill buckets or containers for transfer to a gravity fed filter system. Every year or so, remove the tank inspection cover and pour the appropriate amount* of unscented chlorine in the tank and leave it set for 24 hours before using any water. If possible, it's best to circulate the water in the tank after chlorine is poured in for an hour or so with a small water pump (it's not a showstopper if you don't, but worth the extra effort). I've acquired several of these tanks over the years and believe me—they're getting more expensive by the day!

BE RESILIENT TIP: Implementation guidance available. Reserve your time here* for direct assistance with tank acquisition and setup guidance. I'll show you how to minimize shipping costs and maximize your water resiliency. My implementation support operates through the Sovran Systems Institute, allowing your investment to advance both your personal resiliency and our broader mission.

RESILIENT PATH INSIGHT: The tank from Plastic Mart* I've shown comes with threaded fittings at the top and bottom. PVC fittings and threaded hose bibs must be purchased separately. Put threaded plastic or brass caps on the hose bibs to keep dirt and critters out! If you're interested in acquiring a kit with the valve parts for this tank, you can order the kit here*. Treat this water supply like gold and try not to waste a DROP, it could quite possibly be the only water available for many months until future rainfall or power is restored!

As an alternative for bulk storage, get at least one BPA-free plastic BLUE or BLACK 55-gallon drum that can catch rain water. They can regularly be found on Craigslist or Facebook Marketplace.

The picture above is of a modern, resilient homestead chicken coop, complete with rainwater harvesting, solar power, automated roosting doors, and running water. **NOTE:** The barrels are daisy-chained via brass fittings/hoses on back side near bottom, protected from sun degradation.

DO NOT harvest rainwater off of asphalt shingle roofs! If no non-asphalt roofs are available, use a tarp with the bottom lowest point of the tarp high enough to put a bucket under it: the point where the water's running off the corner or edge (see pic below).

Have two buckets so they can be swapped/filled to transfer to the drum as water's being collected. See a sale on tarps at Harbor Freight? Buy some tarps, some small rope for hanging them and/or large plastic funnels to help in filling the barrel(s)! The tarps will deteriorate if left in the sun, so dry the tarp after each use, fold it up and store for the next time it rains. In fact, if done right, your tarp can double as a dry area for a temporary shelter (if needed)!

NEVER pass up an opportunity to top off the supply! With a steady rain, one or more barrels can be filled in no time!

PFAs*, aluminum salts and other contaminants are now in EVERY drop of rainwater on planet earth. There's just no getting away from it! The filters in the previous paragraphs remove enough of the worst things to radically reduce chances of illness due to contaminated drinking water, including consumption over long periods of time.

PRODUCT RECOMMENDATION: To take your water preps to another level, acquire a portable or house-hold level OZONE water treatment system from Roving Blue*. Their systems use ozone (one of nature's oxidizers) to further neutralize contaminants in your drinking water. The team there have taken practical water preps to a whole new level! Roving Blue's Ozo-pens, GO-3 products and/or Ozo-Pods are outstanding: high-quality, reliable and easy-to-use!

BE RESILIENT TIP: Roving Blue's products ARE NOT FILTERS, they generate ozone to purify water in different quantities, depending on one's needs. Access to relatively clear, contaminant-free water is required before using their products.

Roving Blue's FAQs* are outstanding! A resource-rich library of must-know information about water handling and treatment. **Be sure to pay special attention to the Chapter on Health and First Aid where I highlight a very special reason to have ozone-treated water from Roving Blue!**

In summary, know and be 100% comfortable using personal and household methods of water treatment as fast as possible. Make it a priority and have fun; making it part of a normal routine, conversation piece when company is over or "special day" each month. Take the 1st of the month to only drink water from the gravity-fed water filter system. Buy one extra personal Sawyer Mini to use regularly as part of establishing new habits: learn its flow rate, practice the filtering process, and understand its maintenance requirements. *I use the Berkey for drinking water daily.*

RESILIENT PATH INSIGHT: You can be the invaluable source of water knowledge when the time comes! It's a life-saving skill, provides value to others and is one of the key steps to a high-quality, resilient life!

---

03 - SALT: TURNS OUT IT'S NOT THE EVIL THING WE'VE BEEN TAUGHT

S alt requires a short, critical chapter on its own: next to water, it's that important!

All human beings on earth would quickly perish without salt. Salt is absolutely essential for a body's metabolism and also valuable as a source of micro-nutrients. The type of salt consumed matters. As with anything, the less it's processed, the better.

For example, true sea salt and mined white salt have some nutrients, authentic Himalayan Pink Salt has more and Celtic Salt is nutrient-rich. Believe it or not, there are many more types and sources of salts! Himalayan and Celtic are recognizable, easy to acquire in the USA and enjoyable to eat. It is all still salt, and too much of it is not good either, so use responsibly and what feels right to your body (everyone is unique). You will notice the change almost instantaneously.

While the micronutrients are important, the most important thing to understand about salt is how essential it is to the proper functioning of your core body chemistry and general wellness, in particular the sodium chloride.

There's a reason the #1 go-to solution in hospitals is a saline iv for helping improve general wellness for a physically distressed patient.

Being *"salty"* is literally to be resilient: it is key to maximum resilience.

I don't know about you, but for nearly all of my life I've been taught salt is bad, salt is bad, salt is bad.

I've come to find out the exact opposite is the case.

Salt isn't just life - **salt is the electrical foundation every cell requires to function. What we've been taught is the exact inversion of truth.**

There's MUCH debate about this in institutional circles, but here's my personal experience:

Pickle juice cures leg cramps almost instantaneously (I'm quite sure in large part due to its sodium content)

When I replaced processed sodium from food with pure, high-quality salt dissolved in water, everything changed. My sleep became restorative. My mind cleared. My energy stabilized throughout the day. *This wasn't subtle;* **it was immediate and profound**. Others who made this same shift experienced identical results.

I have much more stamina when I'm intensely working and re-hydrating: drinking a large glass of water and a pinch of Celtic salt mixed in

Taking the importance of salt to another level, I discovered many cultural traditions which further express its value. In numerous traditions worldwide, offering salt (often with bread) to guests represents a fundamental expression of welcome. The Russian tradition of presenting bread and salt to visitors, the Jewish custom of blessing bread with salt on Shabbat, and similar practices in Eastern European and Middle Eastern cultures all reflect this connection between salt and the sacred duty of hospitality.

I recall reading a story several years back about an expedition to the remote Russian island of Kamchatka in the 1950s where researchers discovered a family living off the land in a remote part of the island. The family had fled the conflict in the interior of the Soviet Union during WWII. When the researchers approached the family, one of the adults from the family greeted them first with the following question: do you have any salt?

BE RESILIENT TIP: Throughout history there are a several examples of the weaponization of salt and human beings. Store this in the back of your mind: access to quality salt is an absolute priority. One well known historical example is Ghandi and the great Salt March in India.

I enjoy this salt* for daily consumption:

If you'd like a container like this to put the Celtic salt in for easy access on the kitchen counter, our partner Charming Chisel* can make one for you!

RESILIENT PATH INSIGHTS:

- Acquire a few large bags of high-quality sea salt to have when the eventuality happens and you need it. It stores forever in a cool, dry place. Your knowledge, experience and access to salt will prove to be an invaluable asset!

- If you live close to a body of salt water, it also wouldn't be a bad idea to learn and figure out how to make your own sea salt!

Here's a link* to one example of a bulk salt I'd recommend to have in case of a disruption of access to salt.

04 - A GARDEN OF HARSH REALITIES: RECLAIMING THE LOST ART OF FEEDING YOUR FAMILY

For nearly two decades now, I've slowly "peeled back the onion" on food: growing your own, quality, nutrition, salt, cooking oils, pesticides, toxins, PH*, preservation, and storage. These are so important, each could easily be a chapter itself.

> **BE RESILIENT TIP:** I recommend the 80/20 rule when it comes to food. Do your best to use the following experience and recommendations 80% of the time. If you like vanilla butter cream birthday cake, then eat some once in a while, just not every day. Strive to get to 90/10, but in general enjoy your favorite food and drink and do your best to keep it to a maximum of 20% of the time!

Growing Your Own Food

I don't know about you, but I know only a handful people in my network of a few thousand family and friends who can grow their own food to feed a family. That doesn't say much for our current situation and should be a wake-up call to you. In the early 1900s about 80% of the US population could feed themselves off the land with the resources they had. The other 20% lived in cities and in situations where they could not or would not grow their own food. *Today, those figures are about opposite, where maybe 10 or 15% of Americans can feed themselves and rest cannot!* **Growing food to feed you and your family is much harder than you think.** Pests, animals, weather, soil quality, water quality, extreme weather events, your time and your experience are the factors that make up your ability to grow food effectively: that's a lot of variables!

Food Quality

This is a real problem in America. Dr. Casey Means and her brother Calley Means explain this brilliantly in their book Good Energy*. In short: consuming excessive amounts of processed food is slowly shortening your life and making you sick. The best thing I ever learned and started doing in terms of food quality is to "eat closest to nature." Fewer ingredients on food package labels = less processing. Example: instead of eating an almond cookie, eat some RAW almonds instead, but like anything else, don't over-do it!

Nutrition

Processed foods today have very little nutritional value! **Organic food is worth the price**...you know why? Because what you're not paying now for highest quality food you'll be paying for later in the form of misery, pain, expensive healthcare bills and lower quality of life! Like anything else, don't go crazy and do what you can afford, just know that it matters. Fast food tastes great but is nothing but junk fillers and provides minimal nutrition.

Cooking Oils

In my experience, there are only a few types of oils to use regularly for cooking: high-quality olive*, coconut, avocado or cold-pressed peanut oil. Know your sources! Other cooking oils are highly processed with toxic solvents. Consider them to be in some way, shape or form suspect to your long-term health when consumed in excess. There's a growing amount of research showing this to be the case and *just know that it's not good*. If I'm going to deep fry fish or something else on a special occasion, I use a high quality, organic, cold-pressed peanut oil. Olive and coconut are not suitable for deep frying at higher temps and should be used for low or medium heat pan frying only. Pay attention to every food label to see if there are any oils other than olive, coconut or peanut used in them or in the preparation process. Always keep the 80/20 rule in mind. The next time you look at a bag of "Roasted Almonds" in the store, just check out the label...

Pesticides

I have only one thing to say about them: use them only as a last resort.

Toxins

All things considered; we have it pretty good in the US. If you've ever been to China, India or Mexico, you know why! We're not perfect by any means here in the US, but we are doing better than most. Growing our food in good soil and clean water matters, so do your very best to make sure you're keeping toxins out of the soil, water and air around you.

PH

Each food item we consume has an effect on our body's PH. **I discuss this at length in a later chapter and help you understand why it matters**.

Preservation

With the events unfolding in front of us, food preservation must be a priority for you. The most reliable and practical methods of long-term storage in my experience are canning and freeze drying. There are other methods...however, these two are proven and work best for the importance of this topic. Canning is fairly cost-effective, with freeze-drying being more expensive to get started, but freeze-drying is even more cost-effective in the long run if you're doing large volumes of food and looking for improved nutrient preservation and a much longer shelf life. Another thing to consider is learning how to make PEMMICAN*.

The entrepreneur who figures out how to mass-produce high-quality pemmican in the coming years is going to live a great quality of life! Widely used and traded among Native Americans, early American settlers, Aborigines, and other peoples around the world, it is a high-value, highly nutritious, long shelf-life food.

High temperatures, exposure to sunlight and exposure to humidity with ANY type of stored food degrades it quickly. Heat = faster spoilage. Moisture = bacteria growth. Sunlight = oxidization.

Whenever and wherever possible, cool, dark, dry places tend to be the best to store just about everything.

> **RESILIENT PATH INSIGHT:** Grow the simplest things you can with the highest nutritional value and maximum return on your effort. In my experience, a few of them are:
> • Microgreens – (an outstanding source of vitamins, minerals, phytonutrients and fiber)
> • Green leafy plants such as lettuce (great source of Vitamin A and Vitamin K)
> • Potatoes (an excellent source of Vitamin C)
> For the balance of your needs, the reality is:
> • Grow what grows best in your local soils and climate, eat only what you need and preserve/store the rest!
> • Find a local farmer or grower to buy whatever you cannot grow reliably in volume yourself. You'd be surprised how many local growers there are! (Most farmers don't advertise well)

Chickens

If at all possible, get a few chickens to produce your own eggs! I've found the magic number is 4–5 for two people in a household. It's 4–5 because you will lose one every now and then to sickness or predators. Watch over and take care of them—**losing just one or two of them dramatically affects your egg production.** Unless you have a means to readily sell your excess inventory of eggs, having more than this becomes a financial burden with water, feed, coop size, in-fighting and other "chicken dynamics." If you have 4–5, remember that they won't produce eggs forever. Have a strategy and basic plan for refreshing your small flock every few years. Tractor Supply has everything you need to get started and is my "go-to" for anything chicken-related (chicks, starter coops, food, waterers, feeders, etc.). Chickens are relatively easy to maintain and feed. Once they grow to maturity after 16–24 weeks, this many chickens will produce 3–4 eggs per day. For a couple living on a homestead, this leaves you with extra to share with neighbors, barter with or preserve for a rainy day. Add another chicken for each additional family member on the homestead and you'll be in great shape! Fresh eggs are one of the highest quality foods you can eat with an outstanding amount of nutrition and protein. I typically eat 2–3 fresh eggs EVERY DAY.

BE RESILIENT TIP: Do not wash the eggs until you are ready to eat them. Most will be clean, but some will have a small amount of dirt/debris/chicken sh!t on them, but no worries...just handle with care and they will store just fine in any size egg carton. The fresh eggs have a natural coating on them that keeps them edible for several weeks without refrigeration! They will stay fresh even longer with refrigeration. This is an invaluable long-term protein source which requires minimal effort to maintain. Keeping this in mind: take good care of your chickens!

<u>Canning</u>

Even if you're not an avid canner, learn the process and do some for your own benefit and skills development. Get to know someone who is more skilled and does a higher volume, help them in the process and work together to preserve food for you and your family as well, it's a key part of building your RESILIENT PATH. Having your own canning supplies will make things that much more convenient and cost-effective when the time comes. Buy mason jars whenever you can. Ollies, Walmart and other chain stores regularly have great deals on them.

<u>Freeze Drying</u>

If you have the financial means, time and desire, buy a commercial-grade freeze dryer!

PRODUCT RECOMMENDATION: Harvest Right* is the gold standard of food freeze dryers. Their products and customer service are outstanding and their products speak for themselves. I actually have their first-generation unit and they've come a long way in feature upgrades, user experience and maturity of their software. Ever had a freeze-dried marshmallow? Lucky charms, eat your heart out! There's mountains of information and experience out there and here's some tips on what I've found works best: Get an extra set of drying trays so you can have another set of prepared food ready to go in the dryer as soon as it's done. Once you've finished preparing the next batch, put the trays with food in your conventional freezer to give the freeze dryer a head start before the next cycle is ready to start. Use disposable, food-safe parchment paper on the bottom of your tray or re-usable tray liners. This saves time and effort with cleanup between cycles. The oil-based vacuum pumps are loud, messy and in general, a pain in the a$$. Spend the extra money to get the oil-less pump! Have a dedicated spot in your kitchen, or build/buy a dedicated working table on casters with cabinets underneath, the freeze dryers are VERY heavy and awkward. You don't want to have to move it!

The freeze dryers have LONG process times and are not quiet. If you're a light sleeper, you will want to set up your freeze-drying equipment and process in another room or just sleep somewhere else while it's running! To maximize shelf life, it's best to: use air-tight jars for food you're going to eat in the not-too-distant future. Vacuum-sealed mylar bags with an oxygen absorber packet in them are your most cost-effective method for long-term storage (stored in the right storage conditions, as much as 25 years) The freeze dryer does one thing well: it removes the maximum amount of moisture from the food. Moisture combined with anything organic equals bacteria and rot. Make sure your freeze-drying output is quickly packaged and protected from any re-absorption of moisture.

BE RESILIENT TIP: all those extra eggs you're getting from your chicken coop? Cook and freeze dry them!

One other thing to consider freeze drying is fish, especially if you are fisherman! Other lean meats are compatible with freeze drying, but the fattier the meat, the more risk of spoilage over time. Meats are especially important long-term for the protein and nutrients. Freeze dried in small chunks or strips, it makes an ideal addition to soups and salads or as a snack.

Water-based Growing Systems

I highly recommend hydroponic growing systems of any kind and am a huge fan of the leafy vegetable growing results produced by the Tower Garden* grow systems.

(LEFT) freshly planted starter plants. (RIGHT) 30 days of growth!

BE RESILIENT TIP: Make sure you have an automatic watering valve and hose connected to the system so it stays topped off with water. On a hot day it will consume several gallons of water for this kind of growth! You'll need to also make sure you're keeping up with the food & nutrients with the new water added. Lastly, if at all possible, make sure you have a spare pump and have it connected to an outlet that has a generator backup or that you have an alternate power source in case of an extended outage lasting a day or more. You will lose your crop if it goes without water circulation for 24 hours or more, depending on how hot it is during the day!

Pollinators and Bees

Growing up in a family of beekeepers, I've come to understand the legitimate benefits of honey and more importantly, honeybees. Honeybees are one of our essential pollinators and we humans are dependent on their ability to pollinate. Do everything you can to protect and support their ability to thrive and multiply. Pure honey, has the following benefits:

- a natural, highly compatible sugar for your body and important for diabetics (especially in an emergency, if sugar is needed)

- High in antioxidants

- Aids in burn and wound healing

- Consuming a small amount of locally harvested honey helps tame allergy symptoms for those who suffer from seasonal hay fever, pine pollen, etc.

- A half or full teaspoon of honey mixed with warm water, helps suppress coughs for young, sick children (never give honey to a child under 1 year of age!)

NOTE: Honey is on the acid side of the equation when maintaining your body's PH! **I discuss the importance of body PH in a later chapter.**

As pollinators, they help our gardens grow and will help keep us fed!

RESILIENT PATH INSIGHT: A massive amount of termicides (for termite control) and other insecticides called neonicotinoids are widely used in the USA for pest control. These pesticides are fatally toxic to bees. If you have to treat or have someone treat a building, be very conscious of this. Heavy rain runoff or other release into the surrounding environment will kill your hives nearby or naturally occurring bees in your immediate area.

05 - BUILT TO FAIL: THE HIDDEN CRISIS IN AMERICAN HOUSING RESILIENCE

T he evidence is starting to show: most common modern building methods and insurers don't support long-term sustainability or resiliency! *This will become abundantly clear in the years ahead.* In fact, with mountains of evidence*, and some recent examples*, I can easily prove it.

The current construction market consists of well-established material/supply/installation company monopolies with methods of construction that leave little room for real innovation unless it supports the existing, highly-leveraged construction-financialization model. This is why innovation in this sector seems "stuck." I've collaborated with numerous technology and brick & mortar solution partners with legitimate, high-value, economically viable business models. Each of them has struggled for years to get any real traction or attention from investors, developers, AEC firms, or GOs. Nothing, Nathan, Nada for true innovators in this space. As you'll see in the following experience, *my journey through discovery and problem solving for shelter has been nothing short of good, bad and ugly*!

It's a heavy subject and not an easy problem to solve. So much so, I dedicated over 15 years of my life to solving it: in the form of time, money and effort to create a viable solution*. While not for everyone in every situation, it's perfectly suited for applications such as remote cabins, forest ranger stations, churches, municipal buildings, homes & hospitality venues for disaster-prone real estate, key infrastructure buildings and high-value item storage buildings. In fact, in a later chapter, I elaborate more on this shelter solution's key role in creating viable communities of the future. Let's dive into the situation and solutions.

Insurance

Don't kid yourself, the current property and casualty insurance market in the US has failed financially (and is likely insolvent). What you're witnessing now in the State of FL for example, is a slow-motion train wreck of insurers scrambling to figure out how to default on contracts which most customers have paid premiums for decades, while they shift funds to business-lines they believe they can salvage. Why else would Allstate and State Farm stop underwriting policies in California, one of the TOP TEN economies in the WORLD! In 2022, Allstate and State Farm announced they were no longer going to issue business or homeowner's property insurance policies in the State, due to the unpredictability of "climate change" and their inability to effectively assess risk*.

State-based insurance funds like the Citizens Property Insurance Corporation of Florida* are being created as a band-aid to maintain confidence in the current property insurance model. CA recently announced a similar program* and insurers like Allstate and State Farm are considering re-entering that market again (if they haven't already). The State insurance programs claim they are not taxpayer-funded, but I bet if you peeled back the onion, they are nothing but stealthy bailouts for failed business decisions (remember 2008?). The past and ongoing financial losses in the insurance sector are just too big.

HOMEOWNERS INSURANCE LAWSUITS

Rest of U.S.   Florida

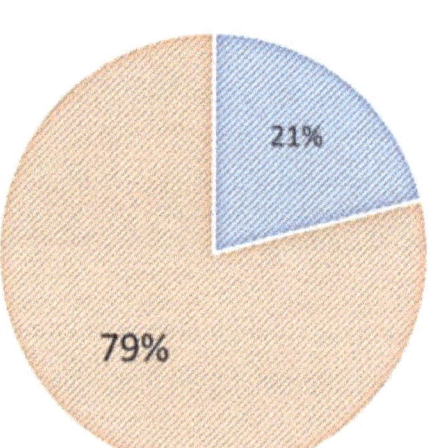

The chart above reflects the proportion of homeowners' property insurance lawsuits as of January 2023 in the US as compared to one state: Florida. What's wrong with this picture?

I'm 100% confident in the math. These State programs are also going to fail in the not-too-distant future, if they haven't already. The fact is we're quickly approaching a point where the system breaks and then we're going to be forced to do things differently. It's like any other decision in life: do I endure the uncomfortable pain and reality now on my terms or do I put it off to a later date while the problem continues to get worse and it happens on someone else's terms?

Water Damage

After a hurricane or flood, did you know that more than 80 cents of every dollar are spent on replacing, rebuilding or repairing damage due to water? A large portion of this staggering amount is spent on the shelters we live and work in. We're talking about drywall, insulation, wood trim, wood sheathing, carpet, tile, appliances, air conditioning systems, computers, fixtures, wiring, repainting, personal belongings and much more. It's such a big problem, solving this problem alone makes a huge dent in righting the ship! Oh, wait, yeah, I forgot…we've already spent trillions of dollars to build our homes and businesses in an unsustainable way and continue to build them back the same way!

Builders

I've tried speaking and working with more than a dozen custom and high-volume builders across the country in the last several years. You're not going to incentivize or convince them to do anything different that doesn't fit into their current way of doing things. As it stands right now, their margins are what they are and they're confident they can continue to make money as is. They're not going to change unless forced to through supply chain issues or other significant product improvements which improve current profitability models.

Utilities

The US now has a large and growing portion of power utility providers which are private, for-profit providers*. In some regions, more than 60% of customers receive electricity from them. Publicly Owned Power Utilities* still exist and provide their customers with exceptional service and power bills that are on average as much as 13% lower than privately owned companies. Public utilities still dominate the water utility space, but that is changing rapidly with the woes of aging infrastructure and retiring staff.

> **BE RESILIENT TIP:** Where's your blind spot? Those private utility providers have ZERO incentive to expedite the restoration of your service or make any changes that don't improve their profitability!

Monopolies hate competition. They've lobbied for decades and continue to lobby to create tighter legislation in EVERY state* of our union which restricts your use of "competing solutions;" rainwater collection, cisterns, next-generation septic tanks, communications and off-grid power sources.

Cash Flow

When disasters happen, **cash flow stops**. Whatever solution you or your community ultimately decide to embrace and invest in, make absolutely sure there's at least ONE sustainable and resilient shelter in the equation which supports minimizing the disruption of cash flow for local small businesses: in the form of dry storage, un-disrupted electricity, un-disrupted communications, a store of potable water and a waste water treatment system. The local businesses and community can rally around this resource and begin the restoration of services and commerce in the broader community quickly. Without this, you are completely dependent on outside "forces" which control your outcome! Doing this around a church or fellowship-sponsored resource is best, and I discuss this later in the chapter on "Community."

Fire

I'll cover this topic much more in a later chapter, but important I touch on one concept briefly here—**What's the easiest way for you to lose everything you've invested in to achieve a sustainable and resilient life? Fire.**

Just look at the show Homestead Rescue* as an example.

> **BE RESILIENT TIP:** Whatever you do, you must have shelter and provisions for fire prevention or fire resilience.

I'll end the fire topic with an important question: In just the last few hundred years, how were people in thousands of African villages, Native American tribes, early American settlers, Civil War armies, and entire cities during the great wars forced to move when some antagonist said they had to go?

They were burned out*.

Weather

Weather is not an exact science, which is why in my next life, I'm going to be a weatherman and get paid for being wrong much of the time! It's not their fault. Based on the data I have and years of setting proper expectations with my colleagues, our weather is going to continue to change unexpectedly over large regions of the country and world. In order to be sustainable, our future communities must begin to introduce economical, highly resilient buildings into the mix. If not, those communities will fail and their residents will be forced to move*. Any solution from here is going to be accomplished by you making a decision that you're not going to spend your time, energy and hard-earned money on something that's not going to last. These decisions and actions, one household at a time, are the "bridge" to a future model of doing things, all while doing our best to economically salvage and re-use whatever possible from the investments already made!

> **PRODUCT RECOMMENDATION:** If you'd like to add some uniqueness, circularity, and nostalgia to a project by incorporating de-constructed or pre-used materials into an existing or new building, reach out to Larry LaMotte at ReCapturit*. Larry* is a leading voice and innovator in the space. This simple action, even if it's a single door, plumbing fixture, electrical fixture or piece of furniture, makes a difference towards legitimately improving your community or regions' sustainability!

Shelter is real estate. The world of real estate, insurance, construction, finance, contractors and materials is not going to stop tomorrow, but other variables in the real estate market are changing rapidly and will drive an involuntary change towards simpler, sustainable and resilient building methods in the coming years. To do anything else will be economically non-viable. It's in your best interest to be ahead of the curve, since statistically upwards of *90% of independent wealth has been made or is generated from real estate-related investments*! It's important that if you're going to invest in any real estate as a long-term investment, especially improved real estate, you make informed decisions about the sustainability and resiliency of the property to assess its true value. Today, there is no real guide to building resilient and sustainable shelter which helps you to simply understand the problems we face and what solutions are available for the path forward. For starters, I challenge you to find a consistent, objective definition of the word "sustainable building" and "resilient construction" anywhere on the internet. Wait, what? All we've heard for the last decade is "sustainable" this and "resilient" that. *Definitions do not exist for the average American in a commonly known and referenced standard.*

Yes, there's LEED Certification and Energy Star. Well intended, but the reality is they haven't moved the needle with proper incentives to result in widespread adoption or objectively sustainable and resilient buildings! If you're not in the construction industry, can you name one building which you know of that is "LEED certified" and if so, what that means to you in terms of benefit from actual sustainability or resiliency? You're starting to understand why this has been such a good, bad and ugly experience! Practically speaking and using my experience as a barometer, a reasonable definition for each of these when balancing cost with performance in today's rural real estate market means that:

"Sustainable" = any occupiable building design economically viable in terms of total build cost and operational cost for the next 50+ years where the number of occupants conforms to current residential and/or commercial building codes.

"Resilient" = Able to withstand extreme weather in the form of 1/2" or less size hail stones, Winds of 120mph or less, floods under 8' in flood prone areas and minimal to zero long-term disruption of essential services like power, water, communications and waste water treatment in the event of a natural disaster.

Legitimately sustainable and resilient shelter using the basic definition above is made possible from these few key factors:

1. Energy consumption and efficiency: Determining requirements by calculating the cost to generate electricity using "off-grid" methods like solar, hydro, geothermal, or other source, without utility power. It doesn't mean you can't use utility power. If you did, you could just use it as a backup or supplemental power source, not your core, essential needs. If "green energy" is as good as the messaging says, then why not?

2. Consistent power: essential mechanical systems require reliable electricity—Heat, A/C, refrigerator, and other appliances. The reality is that without consistent power, in 3-5 weeks the local economy ceases to exist and you're typically forced to re-locate when you experience a catastrophic, extended outage due to; a natural or man-made disaster, a shortage of replacement transformers, wires or poles or a shortage of manpower. Many examples exist in recent history of disruptions forcing people to re-locate: western NC, Ukraine, SW FL.

3. Extreme weather resilience: design features preventing damage from extreme weather events in excess of the reasonable definition above

4. Fire prevention: Design features preventing damage from an exterior fire

5. Water damage prevention: Permanent, intentionally designed protection from water damage

---

BE RESILIENT TIP: Case in point, there are ZERO mass produced off-grid solutions available today which economically compete with on-grid US utility power rates: rates which average 13.7 cents per kWh.

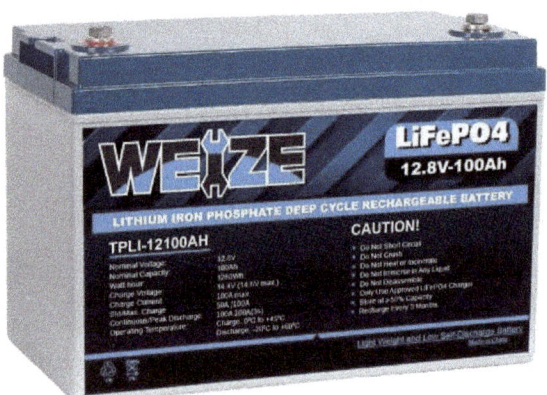

This is an example of one of the more cost-effective, modest-quality lithium batteries made in China.

The math: 100Ah @ 12.8V = 1280 Watts or 1.28 kWh of power storage in this WEIZE lithium battery with a cost of $279.99. The cost per kWh is 218.74 DOLLARS! Compare this to the on-grid cost per kWh of 13.7 CENTS and you quickly begin to understand why on average, only a small percentage of residential solar power systems in the US have battery backup: it's the cost of the batteries! Batteries are just one component of an off-grid solution.

Solar panels, wind turbines, cables, land/real estate, power regulation equipment, power inversion equipment, time, manpower and experience are all additional expenses in the off-grid equation! Why is no one talking about this elephant in the room? Oh, that's right...*because it's an elephant in the room*, and people don't like talking about elephants in the room. As a homeowner, unless you have lots of money to spare, or a legitimately sustainable and resilient building, the math doesn't work. Many thanks to Will Prowse and his YouTube channel* for his invaluable deconstruction, evaluation and assessment of this product and so many others!

RESILIENT PATH INSIGHTS: Here's things to keep in mind and questions you should be asking yourself about your existing and/or new shelter (improved real estate) investments:

- **Property insurance you're paying for on any building(s) quite possibly will not perform as assumed, unless you intimately know it's terms and conditions and have had any ambiguity clarified in writing by the insurer**—you cannot blindly assume property insurance will be reliable in the future, especially in FL, so plan for it

- **Instead of paying for more insurance, intelligently invest in upgrading the existing building or new project to improve basic sustainability and resiliency**: insulation upgrades, high efficiency HVAC, standing seam metal roof, storm shutters, solar power and electrical system upgrades

- **Does the building have the potential to be cost-effectively upgraded with better wall and roof insulation?**

RESILIENT PATH INSIGHTS (CONT'D):

- **Pay very close attention to any prospect of a weather event being able to cause significant water damage to your building(s), especially drywall.** There is high potential for financial loss here!

- **Do the doors in the structure have wood or wood-fiber frames that are prone to rotting or damage by pests?** Future replacement will be cost-prohibitive

- **Are your windows made of wood?** Future replacement will be cost-prohibitive

- **Are your windows single-hung, double-hung or horizontal sliding?** These and sliding glass doors are prone to major seepage from wind-driven rain, resulting in interior water damage and future mold problems. Casements or awning-style windows are best, but storm shutters are a better overall solution in storm-prone areas!

- **Is any part of your exterior made of steel, brick, or concrete materials?** These increase building resilience to weather damage, in particular, external fire threats

- **In the right geography and local conditions, solar power will work as a primary power source in well-insulated, high-quality buildings.** When done correctly, this legitimately improves your sustainability and resiliency overall!

> **BE RESILIENT TIP:** You must understand it's going to be increasingly difficult if not impossible over time to find reliable, skilled tradesman to maintain what you have, so, have spare parts, invest in higher-quality, reliable, long-lived equipment AND find a dependable tradesman to work with in your area. It's wise to invest in these local trade businesses—by contributing to their success, you support long-term resiliency for both of you!

There are no silver bullets and there are no miracle workers—**only token gimmicks and more lipstick on the same pig to make it look "different."** These are simply efforts to extend the existing financialization schemes in real estate. *The reality is that much of the shelters built in the USA and around the world are not built for sustainability or resiliency,* **they were built to make the builder/developer profit or simply what was available to make do.** There are exceptions, but they are the minority. There is no fixing a shelter that's un-fixable without substantial investment and time: this is where building your resiliency in other areas counts. Where your neighbor might be not as prepared, you can be and vice-versa!

As I discuss in a later chapter, the greatest quality of life for you will most likely be in a community with a diverse population of other prepared people! Use this new knowledge about shelter as a way to create value for your family, friends, and neighbors, especially in times of need. The future belongs to those who act now and have valuable resources to rally around, adapt, and make it through! This is also one of the reasons the Sovran Systems Institute* (SSI) was formed. It consists of systems architects who understand complex, resilient and sustainable systems, both technical and natural. The Institute is the rally point for those with the intention and value to contribute to creating the new resilient systems to replace the fragile, mismanaged and failing systems currently in place. What makes SSI different? **SSI's methods preserve the value in what exists, and simply transform it into what's next.**

06 - THE SUPER BALL TUMOR: WHAT MY BRAIN SURGERY REVEALED ABOUT HEALTH RESILIENCE

A fter clean, uncontaminated water, salt, food and shelter, your next priority is your general health and first aid skills! When I say "Health," I'm referring to physical, mental and spiritual. Like anything else in life, *imbalances and deficiencies lead to poor performance or failure.*

If your immune system is deprived of salt, certain vitamins and quality water, at some point you'll probably catch a cold, contract the flu or develop another illness. I'm going to focus on physical, but will share some observations and suggest paths to mental and spiritual resilience as well.

Physical Health

I can't emphasize this enough—**VITAMIN D (D3) is the literal foundation of your body's immune and repair system**. You get it only in one of three ways: Exposure of your skin to sunlight (specifically Ultraviolet B), Vitamin D3 supplements or particular foods. Try putting on swim trunks and laying in the sun for 20-30 mins on a chase lounge or flat surface in the late morning or early afternoon, first on your back, then on your stomach for another 20-30 mins. Do it with no music or distractions...after doing this a few times, it starts to feel almost like you're a battery being re-charged! I've done it for years and it's done wonders for my general health and well-being. If you do a little homework, you'll find that one of the keys to the world getting past the Spanish Flu pandemic of the early 1900s was Vitamin D. Even the smallest increase in Vitamin D levels in your body is beneficial. Late in the Spanish Flu pandemic, hospitals started moving their patient beds outdoors on sunny days and VOILA. People started getting better! This was in large part due to two things: having patients outdoors did give their skin some exposure to sunlight AND the UV light rays from the sun kill pathogens like the Spanish flu.

> **BE RESILIENT TIP:** I don't worry about contracting the flu or a cold by grabbing the handle of a grocery cart that's been outside; it's had plenty of UV exposure to kill any germs and bacteria on the handle! A noisy or bumpy wheel on the cart however, is an entirely different matter!

As my closest colleagues know, I am rarely sick...and if I have an injury or illness, I tend to recover quickly! I pay very close attention to my exposure to the sun and Vitamin D3 supplement intake. You should too. Guess what happens when you put sunscreen on your skin when you're on a beach vacation? You shut off your skin's ability to convert the sunlight to Vitamin D. Coupled with excessive alcohol and eating poorly when you're on vacation, it's a recipe for getting sick! Try this next time you're on vacation or at the beach: spend the first 20 minutes in the sun with no sunscreen, then put your sunscreen on. Too much of anything is not good, including sunlight, so use sunscreen, hats and cover up as needed to prevent damage to your skin.

BE RESILIENT TIP: Your skin is the largest organ of your body and quickly absorbs anything it's exposed to! Educate yourself on the toxic ingredients of liquid sunscreen and avoid ingredients like oxybenzone, octisalate, octocrylene, and homosalate, which are all absorbed into your body.

If your blood has less than 20 nanograms per milliliter (ng/mL) of Vitamin D saturation, you're very prone to illness and poor healing. There are VAST opinions in the medical and professional world about healthy vitamin D levels so I'm simply sharing my decades of personal observations and study which have resulted in an outstanding quality of life and minimal need for "health" and pharmaceutical industries except in the event of something catastrophic (bone break, ruptured appendix, etc.).

Here's an analogy to emphasize how Vitamin D works in your body. Much like a bricklayer needs knowledge, experience, physical ability, bricks and mortar to build a building, Vitamin D also has essential complementary components to work best and support good health and re-construction in your body. They are Calcium, Vitamin K2, Vitamin A and Vitamin E. Applying the bricklayer analogy, Calcium is the BRICKS and MORTAR. Vitamin K2 is the physical bricklayer which knows how to physically place the bricks and mortar (Calcium) in your body. Without K2, calcium often gets deposited in your arteries, which is not good for long-term circulatory and heart health. When a K2 supplement is taken with Vitamin D3 and Calcium, the Vitamin K2 "instructs" the Vitamin D to put the calcium in the best places in your body, namely your bones, teeth, etc. Think of Vitamin A and Vitamin E as the training and hands-on experience the bricklayer needs to know how, what and where to use all of these to build the strongest structure possible. These vitamins (A, D, E, K2) and minerals (Calcium) all work together in harmony as the literal "foundation" of your body's ability to repair itself, fight disease, maintain strong bones, maintain strong vision and much more! The D3, K2, A and Calcium are "fat-soluble" vitamins and best taken with meals, especially in the morning or midday. Avoid taking on an empty stomach.

I strongly recommend at least once a year (late fall is best) to get your blood tested for Vitamin D saturation to ensure you're taking the proper amount of Vitamin D3 supplements and/or getting an appropriate amount of sun exposure. In my experience and research, anything above 50 ng/mL of Vitamin D is great with 70 or more being ideal. As always, moderation is best, so don't overdo it! I recommend blood work in the late fall since many of us live in Northern latitudes and don't get much sun exposure during the winter months. Having your blood tested during this time will give you a general indication of how much Vitamin D3/etc. you should be taking to maintain your immune system over the winter. I always wondered growing up why I got terrible colds and flu over the late fall or winter months! Once I discovered the "secret combination" above, it all made perfect sense.

> **RESILIENT PATH INSIGHT:** Much of the supplements industry products are tainted with chemicals and other undesirable ingredients due to the fact that their raw materials are sourced from China and India. Buyer beware. My recommendations with links in this chapter are from sources I know and trust. While they might not be perfect, they are far better than alternatives. Be diligent!

Keeping it simple, here's one of the best ways with a good balance of several essential vitamins to supplement D, A, K and E: DAKE from Suppgrade

Labs*. You'll notice the link above includes Vitamin E, which also works with Vitamin D3 to support your immune system and deal with chronic stress, called "oxidative stress." Magnesium is a key part of your diet and overall health. Think of magnesium as the "great regulator" of your body's systems: Nerves, muscles, blood glucose, blood pressure and DNA/RNA synthesis to name a few. *Magnesium is best taken at night*; it helps with sleep and a general "recharge" of your body for the next day. This works great for me and noticeably improved my sleep at night: Magnesium 101 from Suppgrade Labs*.

BE RESILIENT TIP: Caffeine consumption via coffee, energy drinks and soda deplete the minerals and nutrients in your body, especially Magnesium! Be mindful of this and make sure you're moderating your intake so as not to overly deplete your body and increase your vulnerability to illness.

Vitamin C, like Vitamin D in particular, is essential to your overall health and has an interesting *"history of mystery"* I'd like to briefly share with you. Scurvy*, the result of Vitamin C deficiency, is a dreadful disease. Often occurring with malnutrition in general, even today it can in some way affect up to 45 percent of refugees. Vitamin C is not stored in the body, so we as humans require constant replenishment, typically in the form of fruits, vegetables and leafy greens. Before the late 1700's and the discovery of and broader understanding of Vitamin C being the cure, Scurvy was prevalent among global populations and often a common cause of death. Remember all the Pirate movies and shows with the reference to SCUUUURRRRVVVVY? For centuries, scurvy was prevalent among sailors on journeys across the oceans for extended periods of time, usually a month or more. The good news is scurvy is not anything to truly worry about in our modern society, unless something catastrophic happens and you run out of nutritious food or supplements. I discuss ways to make sure you're doing what's necessary for sustainability and resiliency of your food supply in a later chapter. Your body has a great way of handling Vitamin C, so it's very hard to overdose. I have a big frame at 6'5" and 270 lbs. and take anywhere from 1000 to 2000 mg per day. Liposomal Vitamin C is ideal. I don't catch colds and am fortunate to have a strong stomach and regular digestive system. Signs you're taking too much Vitamin C are nausea, diarrhea and digestive discomfort. As with anything, excess is not good, so take it responsibly.

Me being aware of the REAL benefits and proper amounts of Vitamin D3 and Vitamin C in my diet has changed my quality of life profoundly for the better. I'm not perfect and do get sick, but it's a rare exception—usually due to neglecting something or unusually high stress from excessive travel or lack of sleep.

BE RESILIENT TIP: It's valuable to have on hand and understand the benefits of one of these 3 powerful antivirals that work quite well with your natural immune system instead of relying on overly-prescribed pharmaceutical antibiotics which negatively affect your gut biome*:

- N-acetyl-L-cysteine (NAC)*

- Quercetin*

- Ivermectin*

RESILIENT PATH INSIGHT: If you know anyone who works on septic tanks or at the municipal wastewater treatment plant, you may have heard that one of the things they see most in their experience working with wastewater is undigested vitamins! If you're going to spend the money on vitamins, buy them in quality and the ideally digestible format. Anything else is a waste of time, money and potential health benefit.

The SECOND most profound thing that improved my general health and resiliency to stress was managing my body's PH! Oh, you didn't know this was "a thing" you should manage? *If you've ever owned or managed the chemistry of a swimming pool or hot tub, you'll know THE most important thing to manage to maintain water quality is PH (Acid/Alkaline balance).* If you don't, it goes to heck-in-a-hand-basket pretty quickly...algae, bacteria, yuck! Your body is on average more than 60% water, and like swimming pool chemistry, must be maintained or it will be yuck too! Kind of ironic the earth's surface is covered by approximately the same percentage of water as in our bodies. A funny coincidence, eh?

You may be telling yourself, bah, I don't have to do this! Well, let me share at least why it mattered to my health and quality of life. Sadly, I experienced divorce after 17 years of marriage. Stressful is an understatement. *Chronic stress is one of the greatest slow killers and shows up in people in different ways*: cancer, chronic illness, skin issues, etc. Minimizing and eliminating chronic stress plays a big part in resilient health and quality of life. Several years prior to my divorce, I learned of the importance of managing your body's PH. In fact, did you know there's lists available that show you which foods and liquids you consume have an acid or alkaline reaction with your body chemistry? Here's one example:

Acid/Alkaline Food Chart*

Where's your blind spot?

I'm a living example of what happens when you proactively work to ensure your body's PH is slightly alkaline by implementing a "micro-adjustment" to address a blind spot. I survived brain cancer because of the micro-adjustment I made to consistently manage my PH! In 2013 (not long after my divorce was finalized), I had sudden chronic ringing in my left ear. Since this was completely unexpected, I went to a highly recommended ear specialist in my area for a checkup. As part of the protocol and my symptoms, he recommended I get an MRI to make sure he had the full picture for diagnosis. Well, a week after my MRI and with a follow-up appointment, I received the bad news—I had a golf ball-sized tumor next to my brain stem! This is what was affecting my hearing, it's called a vestibular schwannoma, or "acoustic neuroma." Not typically fatal, but mine was in a very bad spot and had *grown into my brain stem*. Yes, yikes. Turns out, this tumor had been growing for more than twelve years in my head! This size is considered stage IV, so I had to act quickly because of the potential impact to my long-term health and quality of life.

In the only way I know to explain it, "divine circumstances" led me to a unique, pioneering surgeon who did the surgery endoscopically. Much like endoscopic knee surgery, this type of procedure would likely minimize the impact to my quality of life and reduce my recovery time to less than a year (the traditional procedure had an expected recovery time of up to 2 1/2 years!). BTW...I have many witnesses to these life-changing "divine" events. *I figured out why on August 22nd of 2013 this was the surgeon who must operate on me:* **my case was truly unique**. My surgery took nearly twice as long compared to more than three thousand prior patients (a normal surgery was 4 1/2 hours). Why did mine take so long? After the surgery when I arrived in recovery, the doctor, to my surprise, asked me "Mr. Atkinson, what do you do different?" He asked me this because a normal tumor that he works on is the consistency of Jello and is not difficult to remove. *He said mine was the consistency of a super ball.* This is why my surgery took so long. I had a super ball grown into my brain stem! His surgical gifts helped him very carefully cut away and remove the hard, rubbery pieces of the tumor located more than 17CM deep in my head—without rendering me permanently disabled in some way! *My surgeon was a literal godsend.* For various reasons I cannot disclose his name, but if you, Dr. S. ever read this book, know that I'm eternally grateful to you!

My tumor was the consistency of a super ball because it had calcified from consistent management of my body's PH in the several years prior to the surgery. It was the only major change in my lifestyle that would have done that. **Tumors are acidic and cannot survive in a slightly alkaline environment, so my tumor died**. Normal, healthy cells maintain a slightly alkaline environment, typically hovering around a pH of 7.35 to 7.45. In stark contrast, cancer cells create and thrive in an acidic microenvironment, with pH levels dropping to approximately 6.5 to 6.9. After much discomfort due to 24x7 VERTIGO and complete inability to walk for more than 4 months, I made a full recovery with one exception: I lost the hearing in my left ear, which is not uncommon with this type of tumor and surgery. *Now you know one of the real secrets to maintaining a resilient immune system.* **You must manage the PH of the water in your body**! How do I manage mine? Simple: about a tsp of lemon juice in an 8 to 12 oz. glass of water every morning immediately after I wake up. I can't recommend it enough to people whose bodies respond well to citrus (some don't so you'll have to find what works best for you!) If you do this, be sure to rinse your mouth/teeth with pure water after you drink the water and lemon juice to rinse away any remaining citric acid.

BE RESILIENT TIP: Infections are bacterial and viral in nature. Depending on what type it is, it will respond differently in acid, neutral or alkaline conditions. Understand that your first, best defense against viruses and bacteria is a healthy immune system and a well-balanced, stable, gut and microbiome. Did you know there's a healthy debate raging about the negative effects of mouthwash on the healthy microbiome in your mouth?

RESILIENT PATH INSIGHTS: Everything you ingest or expose your physical body to has an effect on you, but don't worry! Focus on what you have control over...which is quite simply:

- what you eat and drink

- what and who you listen to

- your immediate physical environment, such as air quality

- who you invest time with and what you do with that time together

Here's another reason why a resilient immune system and quality of life should be an imperative: *America and the rest of the world's population in developed countries experienced an explosion in excess mortality starting in 2020.* In fact, several insurance companies underwriting disability insurance policies have sounded the alarm in recent years due to this disturbing increase*. Ed Dowd and the team at www.phinancetechnologies.com* continue to provide us a glimpse of what to expect in the future and the implications of increased mortality rates around the world. Their work is outstanding and I encourage you to incorporate the data from their evolving research and interviews into any/all of your preparedness plans!

RESILIENT PATH INSIGHT: Due to the long-term, civilization-altering trend of excess mortality globally, I intensely researched the excess mortality origins and patterns. What I discovered was a systematic compromise of information architecture itself. The institutions we've trusted to validate truth have been captured by the very interests they claim to regulate.

For example, as a father, SIDS was always a concern with my young children. My research revealed that "peer-reviewed" studies consistently show patterns that contradict raw database evidence. This isn't because the data lies, but because the interpretation apparatus has been weaponized. When vaccination was removed as an official cause of death classification in 1979, any vaccine-related fatalities had to be reclassified.

Having built and managed many of the core-data and publishing systems for the American Medical Association as Technical Services Leader, I witnessed firsthand how ICD codes are created, standards are established, and the monopolistic collusion that exists between the association, insurance industry, and healthcare groups nationwide. The structural manipulation makes honest assessment nearly impossible.

> **RESILIENT PATH INSIGHT (CONT'D):** The real issue isn't any single causation claim. The problem is that we can no longer trust the gatekeepers of information to provide unfiltered data. "Peer-reviewed" research has been compromised for decades by funding from biased interests and requires complete re-architecture to restore informational sovereignty.
>
> This extends far beyond health policy. When institutions designed to protect truth systematically obscure it, *sovran* individuals must build parallel systems of verification and validation.

The last major physical health topic I'll cover is your teeth. *If you have any dental issues, get them fixed asap.* You'd be surprised how quickly you can be completely debilitated or even die from what appears at first to be a nothing burger in your mouth! Infection, Cavities, gum issues, root problems, whatever it is, if anything feels out of sorts, get it fixed and be proactive about your gums and teeth!

There's an increasing body of evidence and research happening in the world of human teeth and the mouth biome*. It's looking to have a much greater influence on balance and stability of our bodies than previously known! When the time comes, I'm sorry to say that many of our family and friends will suffer from the lack of access to modern dentistry.

Mental Health

If you're not aware, at the time of this writing, we have a literal mental health crisis which feels like it's everywhere, at every level, like all the parents are away on vacation and the kids have the run of the place. Bad decisions, inconsideration for others, zero situational awareness and general lack of respect for anything or anyone appears to be the current zeitgeist*. But here's what I know: collapse is optional when you have proper structural support.

Most people operate in isolation, making critical decisions without any reliable feedback loop. That's not sovranty—that's structural weakness waiting to fail.

You must have someone in your life who reads signal and structure without distortion. *Someone who mirrors what's actually happening in your field,* **not what you hope is happening.** Some of us have that rare person in our life who tells us the truth without trying to rescue us, but most of us don't have that person with the brutal honesty required for it.

I'm here and able to have written this book because of that person in my life and my own internal pursuit of clarity; both required for true sovranty.

The key is having access to unshakable perspective when your own view gets compromised. Not sympathy. Not comfort. Clear reflection of what's true so you can course-correct before anything collapses. Most people don't have that level of structural integrity in their relationships, which is precisely why they get stuck in patterns that drain their energy and compromise their capacity.

Having witnessed this general lack of that 'unshakable perspective' available today and with my vast experience in technology, systems, entrepreneurship and relationship building, I figured out how to bridge the gap.

Enter Nicole Connor – a brilliant systems mind who shares many parallel resiliency-building experiences in her professional and personal life. Through our work together, we discovered that this type of unshakable perspective and field-reading precision could be systematized, and made available to anyone navigating their path to resilience.

That's exactly why My Resilient Self* exists. **Everyone deserves access to that kind of clarity.** My Resilient Self (MRS for short) provides the uncompromising field mirror that most people lack: someone who can read your signal and structure, identify blind spots before they become costly failures, and reflect what's true so you can maintain forward momentum. It's life-altering to have access to perspective that prioritizes your structural integrity over your comfort—in the form of a resource that's accessible 24 x 7, 365 days a year. Nicole and I figured out *how to use AI to maximize human potential*, **not to render it obsolete, as many aspire to do.**

This is about building proper support architecture for a resilient life - but remember, 'You Get What You Give.' That's not just a catchy tune by the New Radicals*; it's the fundamental law governing energy exchange. The structural integrity you build with MRS depends entirely on the authenticity you bring to each interaction.

Personal responsibility is just that...personal. Take responsibility for each and every one of your actions and make sure you're legitimately and honestly giving consideration to the perspective lenses of others! Elders, parents, siblings, cousins, teenagers, children, neighbors, veterans, teachers, active-duty soldiers, policemen, firemen, etc. Each and every one of them sees the world through a unique lens and deserves consideration! You'll find that as you begin to embrace this consideration, your life is altered for the better, forever. As an example, in my travels through America and around the world, people from every country I've ever traveled to are generally good. As each of us come to these realizations and stop mass stereotyping, I'm confident the world will *rapidly* become a much better place!

> **RESILIENT PATH INSIGHT:** As I've refined use of The Resiliency Code, I've discovered its most powerful feature: it **exposes in-authenticity and dishonesty instantly**. They cannot coexist with structural integrity. In a world where deception masquerades as strategy and manipulation poses as leadership, what could be more essential than a system that reveals truth without compromise?

The Resiliency Code was created from life-experiences which demonstrated that when each of us discovers our own physical, mental and spiritual mis-alignments, we can take action in the form of "micro-adjustments" each day. Small, meaningful changes in an effort to minimize the impact of our failures and provide us the greatest chance to "fail-forward." Failing-forward maintains our growth momentum such that we don't have to "burn out" or "reset" from zero. *That being said, the honest truth is that there are bad apples*: fellow humans which have chemical imbalances, disorders, radical mentors or experiences in their lives, resulting in an incompatibility with society in general. There really is such a thing as psychopaths, sociopaths, murderers, etc. (you get my drift). **Be mindful of this in the years to come**.

Spiritual Health

Our civilization is built on societies which have a common set of beliefs and customs, *this is the literal glue that holds our society together*. Each of us as individuals has a truly unique view of the world (as I shared above), hence, it's necessary to give consideration to others for their beliefs, especially spiritual beliefs. Generally speaking, all people have some sort of common ground to work from. Whatever your belief system is, it is yours, but likely has much in common with others. Divisiveness and intolerance are toxic to a society and culture in general, no matter what your beliefs. **That said, if you're legitimately interested in the greatest quality of life, believe in what deep inside your**

heart feels right, listen to your natural intuition and then collaborate with others to do good things which improve the lives of others.

The greatest crisis we face in the world today is a crisis in leadership. Be the exceptional example and do the right thing regardless of peer pressure or influence. Whether you believe in the Most High or not, doesn't matter...the fact is that there are consequences to each of your actions that affect others and if left unchecked, result in catastrophic events which have occurred throughout history (an outstanding book on this topic is Victor Davis Hanson's recent book: The End of Everything*). Given my personal experiences, I apply the concept of "reasonable doubt" to everything. After all, reasonable doubt is a key element of our criminal justice system in America! If there's reasonable doubt, a conviction is not possible without the legal burden of proof being met! I've seen and experienced sufficient physical evidence to know there is something more than just our physical existence! In fact, I thoroughly enjoy deep philosophical discussions on the topic as part of my journey to understand what I don't know.

In the meantime, I encourage you to seek, learn and understand as much as you can on this topic, *doing your best not to limit yourself to extreme dogmas which demand divisiveness, victimhood and intolerance.* And whatever you do, do not in any way attempt to force your beliefs on someone else! Share your experiences in a collaborative way to improve your quality of life, which ultimately improves the quality of life of those around you and on and on...you get my drift. Consequences are real and I have yet to see one example of a personal judgment which resulted in a benefit to anyone.

First Aid

Take a class in CPR—not online, an actual hands-on class where you learn how to perform compressions and the breathing techniques. **The first place I recommend going to find a class is your local fire & rescue department.** They often hold classes at a very low cost. They are the experts and deal with life and death every day! Learn how not to be squeamish around blood or wounds. You or a loved one's life may depend on it!

> **BE RESILIENT TIP:** Take a fishing trip and hold a bloody fish or actually learn how to clean the fish.

Having grown up in a commercial fishing family and fishing my entire life, I can confidently tell you it definitely helps get over squeamishness around blood. I can typically treat and dress a profusely bleeding wound and if it's not too serious, have a person back in action quickly! Know your personal blood type and blood types of those most important to you. If you ever are mortally wounded and require large amounts of blood, a transfusion is your only hope. You must know that at any given time, you may or may not be able to get blood for a transfusion. The blood supply network in the US is becoming more fragile by the day. Be mindful of situations which could potentially result in deep lacerations, especially in your neck, underarm or groin areas! Quickly address injuries, no matter how insignificant you think it may be. Something insignificant today could be life-threatening in the future without proper supplies and treatment.

> **PRODUCT RECOMMENDATION:** Proper basic supplies: Ionized Silver Gel*, quick-stitch sutures*, gauze*, band aids*, self-adhering bandage wrap* are all must haves in your first aid supplies.

> **RESILIENT PATH INSIGHT:** Remember my reference to Roving Blue products when it comes to first aid? The ozone-treated water produced by Roving Blue products* is the best wound irrigation treatment you could ever use! Abrasions, burns and open wounds will heal in less time, minimize scarring and if done correctly, radically reduce the chance for infection when treated immediately with ozone infused water! I've seen it in action. Incredible results.

07 - SH!T HAPPENS: THE UNCOMFORTABLE TRUTH ABOUT WHERE YOUR WASTE REALLY GOES

O ne thing I've come to observe and understand is that Americans in general are *utterly blind when it comes to the realities of sanitation in our country.*

When I say sanitation, I mean the treatment of human urine and feces. As recent as 2022, 420 million people around the world are still defecating outdoors*. This is a tremendous improvement from the 1B+ which were defecating outdoors at the most recent turn of the century. As a species, we're making great progress here in terms of reducing open defecation. *The real question is, however, in those places where open defecation has all but been eliminated, where does all this sh!t go?* Well, it typically goes one of two places:

- a household or small commercial building's septic system

- a municipal sewer system

Septic Systems

Septic systems are pretty straightforward. A system is typically sized by the local health department and an appropriately sized holding & filtration tank is installed in addition to a leech field*. These systems are pretty low maintenance when installed properly. Other than the occasional pumping-out of solids or electric pump issue*, they're very much out of sight and out of mind.

Municipal Sewer Systems

Municipal sewer systems are centralized processing plants that perform effectively the same process as a household septic system, just on a much larger scale. They remove solids and bring the liquids to a level of purity that is typically safe to discharge back into the environment.

What most people in the USA don't know is that the solids and other sludge removed from the waste stream of a Municipal Sewage Treatment Plant are often taken and disposed of in the following ways:

Application on Agricultural Fields, in Forests and Reclamation Sites (54%)

Landfill (29%)

Incineration (16%)

Composting (1%)

Advanced conversion such as biogas (less than 1%)

Wait, what? **54% is disposed of on farm fields, forests and "reclamation sites?"** Yep—used as "fertilizer." What about the pharmaceuticals and other chemicals we ingest that leave a residual amount in our urine and feces? Is it separated out during waste processing? *Nope.* **The treatment of residual chemicals in municipal waste streams is complex and not entirely comprehensive.** Here's a brutally honest breakdown:

1. Primary Chemical Removal Processes:

- Physical Removal Methods

- Screening

- Sedimentation

- Filtration

2. Chemical Treatment Stages

- Coagulation

- Flocculation

- Chemical precipitation

- Chlorination/Disinfection

Persistent Chemical Challenges:

- PFAS (Per- and Polyfluoroalkyl Substances)

- Pharmaceutical residues

- Heavy metals

- Microplastics

- Endocrine disrupting compounds

Removal Effectiveness:

- Not all chemicals are completely removed

- Current treatment technologies have significant limitations

- Many compounds pass through standard municipal treatment processes

Regulatory Oversight Gaps:

- EPA regulations are often behind emerging chemical threats

- Limited testing for comprehensive chemical profiles

- Agriculture application standards have known weaknesses

Where's your blind spot?

Most municipal waste treatment plants are not designed to comprehensively remove all emerging chemical contaminants. This means residual chemicals are likely entering:

- Agricultural lands

- Groundwater systems

- Food production chains

The brutal truth: Our current waste treatment infrastructure is playing catch-up with industrial and consumer chemical innovation.

BE RESILIENT TIP: Be aware of the sources of your food and water: specifically, the potential of contamination from gaps in the processes above.

RESILIENT PATH INSIGHT: Here's a place where Pause. Prepare. Participate. can be utilized. Pause in order to understand potential risks, prepare appropriate mitigation strategies, and then participate constructively in addressing water quality concerns. There are potential epigenetic consequences to not doing so. Have you ever considered this prior to acquiring a home or place to live?

Additionally, for those of you who have individual septic systems: when the electricity stops for an extended period of time, your septic tank is going to fill up and fill up quickly! Make sure you've got contingency plans for a power source to run your septic tank pump. If you don't, you might find yourself being added to the population of those defecating outdoors!

08 - RADIO SILENCE: BUILDING COMMUNICATION SYSTEMS THAT WORK WHEN EVERYTHING ELSE FAILS

After water, salt, food, shelter, health/first aid and sanitation, communications are your next priority. Without communications, you will be isolated, uninformed, unable to collaborate and unprepared for potentially life-threatening circumstances.

Forget your cellular phone in an emergency, the best way to look at it is as a portable flashlight, glorified calculator or high-resolution camera at most. In fact, should America experience a catastrophic, nationwide emergency or crisis, I strongly recommend you put your "Smart" phone in a GODARK bag* and leave it there permanently. I discuss "why" in a future chapter. You must have two ways to communicate practically:

- **Local**, roughly a mile or less

- **Long distance**, anything beyond a mile.

Short Distance Communications

Acquire a short-range vhf handheld radio for each adult and teenager in your household. If you have them already, great. If not, I recommend The Baofeng UV-5R radio*, a spare battery*, and upgraded antenna*. Keep them fully charged and in a readily accessible place (like a kitchen counter, top of bedroom dresser, garage tool bench or basement window sill). These are line of sight radios and their range is dictated by transmit power and obstructions like trees, buildings, hills and mountains. The movies where you've seen where people talking via two-way radios at distance while underground or inside a building. *The communications are fake.* **It doesn't work that way**! This is why VHF radios are ideal and so widely used for boats on open, flat, unobstructed water! The reality is that with a portable hand-held VHF radio, on average *you're typically going to see reliable communication of a mile or less* where you're outside, on land, with limited obstructions. Testing your radios and being comfortable with reliability over short distances in your area is the best thing you can do for satisfying 90% or more of your communication needs! Familiarize yourself with "CHIRP*" software and how to quickly program your radios with a simple cable* and personalized channels for your situation/family/community.

RESILIENT PATH INSIGHTS:

- Use My Resilient Self* as your guide to basic setup with all considerations for The Resiliency Code.

- When you press the transmit button on your radio, you are sending out a geo-locatable, non-private, broadcast transmission. If you are in a situation where your life is in potential danger and your location is best not known, do not use your hand-held radio and rely on pre-planned, precisely timed and scheduled short communications with your family, friends and neighbors.

Long Distance Communications

Acquire a satellite phone. The reality is, if the situation arises, this is one of the best, practical, reliable methods to effectively talk over long distances when cellular communications are unavailable or unreliable.

PRODUCT RECOMMENDATION:

My preference is the Inmarsat IsatPhone 2*

Experience and Considerations:

The Inmarsat 2 is a cost-effective satellite phone. There's regular specials with our partner Satellite Phone Store. *A sat phone is insurance and an investment.* Imagine the value you'll have to others when only you can communicate with the outside world and your most trusted and reliable information sources with a pool of highly valuable minutes available!

PRODUCT RECOMMENDATION (CONT'D):

Theft: because of the value noted above, it's in your best interest to share the fact that you have a satellite phone with only your most trusted relationships (and imperative to set proper expectations with them as well!)

Know that your satellite phone location is traceable and conversations can be monitored. If necessary, use of communication security protocols is recommended (covered in the chapter on security)

Usability: Sat phones are clear sky devices and must be used outdoors with a clear line of sight to the sky. Just like SirusXM Satellite Radio, when you pass under a bridge, under a tree or go into a parking garage, you will lose signal.

Hand held sat phones will function in all but the worst of weather situations, where you're probably not going to be talking on the phone anyhow! It's a bit clunky like early cellular phones and takes some getting used to, but this keeps just anybody from using it and wasting precious minutes of airtime!

Programming: With an Inmarsat Isat Phone 2 Sat Phone (NOT PHONE VERSION 2.1), programming is still done the old-fashioned way like the original flip phones. Old school...yeah!

Having the phone and having the skills to use it will be an invaluable resource to you, your family and community when the time comes!

I'm sure many of the HAM Radio operators are having kittens now that I haven't explicitly called out dedicated HAM Radio above. Make no mistake, it deserves attention and ham capability is built into my Baofeng recommendation. Note my HAM-specific comments below.

Alternative Communication Technology Comparison

Satellite Internet (Starlink)

Advantages: Comparable cost to a sat phone depending on plan; great performance similar to high-speed internet

Disadvantages: Less portable than a sat phone; health risks of frequency exposure still uncertain; requires 110v power source; specialized cabling needed; traceable location; questionable future availability in conflicts

Satellite Internet Hotspots (non-Starlink)

Advantages: Can still communicate with functioning infrastructure; peer-to-peer software may work even if hosted services fail

Disadvantages: Expensive hardware; high monthly fees; traceable location; uncertain satellite availability in future conflicts

Bivy Stick (Bluetooth Satellite Transceiver)

Advantages: Useful for emergency communication; more cost-effective than a sat phone

Disadvantages: Traceable location; requires a powered, trackable smartphone; uncertain satellite availability in future conflicts

HAM Radio

Advantages: Large operator network exists; short and long-distance communication possible; cost scales with setup complexity; can use without license in emergencies

Disadvantages: Specialized equipment; requires knowledge and experience; needs tall antenna for range; weather can impact communication

BE RESILIENT TIP: Scanners may be useful for monitoring local communications in an emergency situation, but are known to be inconsistent and unreliable at times.

It's entirely possible that depending on the level of disruption and the type of event (solar flare, hurricane, fire, earthquake or other catastrophically widespread disaster), that a "Pony-Express-like" method of long-distance communication may be necessary. I foresee these networks developing organically and regionally, depending on the level of disruption and resources available.

09 - THE DETROIT TIME MACHINE: HOW 1980S VEHICLES HOLD THE KEY TO YOUR FUTURE MOBILITY

R egardless of how you feel about him as a media personality, Tucker Carlson has basic transportation nailed. His daily driver* is a low-tech, manual transmission, 2WD 1987 Chevy Silverado short-bed! During the late 1970s, 1980s and early 1990s, vehicle specifications, standards and build quality in general had one thing in common for many US and some foreign manufacturers like Mercedes Benz: They were built to last.

Not built to last 100,000 miles, just **built to last as long as possible**. Longevity and reliability were the priority back then and must be for your future transportation needs. If you're going to buy something for local, practical, no-frills transportation, buy a late 1980s Chevy pickup truck, preferably with a stock 350, manual transmission, 4-barrel carburetor, 2WD and short or long-bed. 4WD is ok, but understand there are many more moving parts and complexity. There are many other makes and models of that vintage which would probably do just fine, but Chevrolet alone manufactured on average more than 500,000 pickup trucks per year during the 80's.

Where's your blind spot?

Almost one reason and one reason alone...*availability of spare parts**. That generation of trucks is one of the most widely used, after-marketed, simple and reliable ever built. You don't have to go far to see what I'm talking about. Look at Cuba and the cars* they're still driving today which they've driven since the early 60's!

Getting back to the Chevy truck. Yeah, yeah, I know, they're not perfect, but they definitely fit the bill. We could immerse ourselves in the "which manufacturer is better" debate, but why? For sake of resiliency and sustainability, it works and works very well. If any of you can make something different work for you on a local or regional basis, go for it! After all, Ford did manufacture a comparable number of pickup trucks during that time period. In fact, the Ford 351 Windsor is one of my favorite engines! Similar to the Chevrolet 350, it was one of the most widely used in the USA!

As the realities of the real supply chain crisis hit home over the next few years, it will sink-in that we "over-outsourced" our manufacturing overseas and demand will shift from relying on imports to salvage and re-use! Why a pickup truck? Fresh gasoline (as discussed in the next chapter on Electricity & Fuel), will become a highly valuable resource, which means you're going to use it sparingly and load every vehicle to the max with people or materials when you take a trip to town to get maximum value out of the fuel you're consuming. You can't do that as efficiently, or quickly with a 2-door or 4-door sedan! That said, any reliable, mass-produced vehicle you can get spare parts for is going to be just fine for your general, local transportation needs. 80's through early 00's vintage Toyota Camrys, Toyota Corollas, Honda Civics, Honda Accords, Toyota Tacomas, Toyota 4Runners, Toyota Land Cruisers, Honda CRVs, Jeep Wranglers, Ford Broncos, Ford Mustangs, Chevy Caprice Classics and others come to mind.

> **RESILIENT PATH INSIGHT:** Minimal or zero electronics in any vehicle will be the most desirable (such as manual windows and door locks). As the spare parts crisis unfolds over the next decade, being able to service your vehicle yourself or to be able to roll down your windows and lock/unlock your doors reliably is **going to be a real luxury**.

One of the vehicles in my household has manual windows and manual locks...it's priceless when people ride with me and look for the electric window switch to put the window down! I prefer to drive vs. flying whenever possible. My daily driver is a 2007 Dodge 3500 dually with the "Mega cab" and has proven to be outstanding as a travel vehicle. The 2007 models with diesel engines were one of the last model years before complex diesel emissions systems went into "overdrive" (pun intended) and DEF was implemented into the engine emission and exhaust systems. Simpler is always better. Having used the Dodge for more than a decade and 300K miles, I understand why it's the preferred chassis for long-haul medium-duty towing! Reliable, resilient, good power, comfortable to drive and you can get spare parts!

> **BE RESILIENT TIP:** Get to know the local junkyards and other potential places to get spare parts for your vehicles.

Other motorized equipment considerations for a homestead: A skid steer, backhoe or good-sized homestead tractor like a Kubota, Massey Ferguson, Ford, New Holland, Case or other is going to be essential in the coming years. Diesel-powered is preferred, with no DEF if at all possible. Removing stumps, moving dirt, excavating, clearing downed trees, mowing, road maintenance, and other needs are going to make a piece of well-maintained, reliable equipment and skilled operator invaluable.

> **PRODUCT RECOMMENDATION:** A mid-sized Kubota tractor like the L60 series* is outstanding. Knowing several Kubota tractor owners and the manufacturer's reputation for reliability, service, innovation and attachments, it's my go-to brand. For skid-steers, I've owned and operated John Deere, New Holland, and JCB. Based on this experience and hundreds of hours of research, Takeuchi is reliable and others like Bobcat, CAT, and Case have their pros and cons. JCB is my preference, specifically their tracked units—primarily because of visibility, stability and safety from their single-arm lift boom design. A JCB dealer I worked with at one point called JCB skid steers "one-armed bandits"...priceless. Did you know that JCB is the original inventor of the backhoe? Headquartered in SE GA, they continue to demonstrate a leadership position in innovation.

Have several attachments for a skid steer and/or tractor including a bucket, forks, 3-point bush hog mower and 3-point box blade. Fortunately, the fork attachment is generally interchangeable between the skid steer and large farm tractor with front bucket, so you should only have to acquire one. Whatever automobiles and motorized equipment you have, make sure you keep several spare oil-changes worth of engine oil on-hand with plenty of hydraulic oil, hydraulic oil filters, brake fluid, engine oil filters, air filters, fuel filters (gas), diesel fuel filters, pulley belts, spare bulbs and spare fuses for basic maintenance in the coming years.

Also invest in the highest quality car/truck/equipment battery you can afford! I've had great experience with the performance of the AGM (Absorbed Glass Mat) batteries. Expensive, but tough! My jury is still out on lithium car batteries. I'll do a separate post on that at some point on the Sovran Signal YouTube channel*. If financially possible, buy a spare set of tires for your daily driver and store them in heavy duty plastic bags somewhere indoors out of direct sunlight. You'll be thanking yourself you did in the not-too-distant future!

RESILIENT PATH INSIGHTS:

The importance of diesel fuel treatment and fuel storage for this equipment is covered in future chapter—pay particular attention to my comments on DEF "Diesel Exhaust Fluid" and why you should do everything possible to choose diesel-powered equipment which doesn't require it.

Opinions vary, but in my experience, I've had best luck with oil, fuel and air filters made by: WIX, Napa Gold, Bosch, and Fleetguard.

---

10 - WHAT COMES AFTER AI'S FALSE PROMISE: WHY MANUAL SKILLS AND TOOLS WILL DETERMINE WHO THRIVES

Having high-quality tools and knowing how to use them well is going to be the difference between thriving and starving in the coming years. Your access to these tools and a bit of skill will support continuity of things and provide value as a source of income and/or barter. This can range from yard work to appliance repairs.

The push for automation and AI, in large part is due to the demographic and energy crises several developed countries are facing before 2030. These countries are; the US, China, Japan, South Korea and Great Britain to name a few.

Peter Zeihan does an outstanding job articulating this to his readers in the book The End of the World is Just the Beginning* and to audiences around the world in his keynotes, podcasts and other interviews. Authors like Strauss & Howe in the book The Fourth Turning* and The Fourth Turning is Here* affirm what Peter knows as well as provide additional context in how our demographic generations play a major part in demographic cycles. Peter's not perfect, but he's on the mark when it comes to the key data points in demographics and resources. As my colleague Dr. Chris Martenson is so fond of saying: **ENERGY IS THE ECONOMY**.

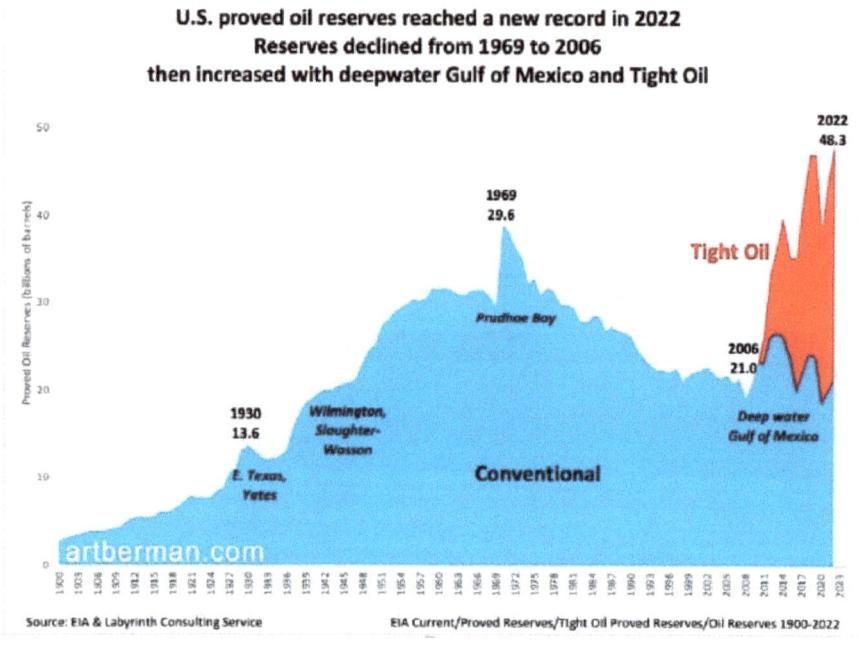

The Permian basin, Eagle Ford, Bakken, Anadarko, Niobrara, Haynesville and Appalachia regions are beginning to slowly roll over and decline at various rates. *We're not going to run out*, **but the explosive growth in shale is going away and starting its slow decline**. What you're now witnessing geopolitically around the world is a mad scramble for resources. We are involved in the Ukraine and Middle East for two reasons and two reasons primarily: *energy and resources*.

The chart above represents US domestic energy production over the last 120+ years.

The US standard of living would be decreasing rapidly today if shale oil doesn't happen. Regardless of how you feel about abiotic oil, conspiracies about oil being a commodity of managed scarcity (like diamonds), the fact of the matter is that since energy is the economy, its availability directly affects our standard of living.

Where's your blind spot?

Every civilization requires a continuous, young, skilled workforce to sustain a population. If you let your birth rate fall below 2.1 births per female in your population, you're not even sustaining what population you have.

In places like China, there is no Social Security like here in the US. *The male children of Chinese families are their social security*. This is why the one-child policy was such a demographic disaster for China. If a family had a girl, it meant the girl would marry and her obligation would eventually be to her new husband's parents, not her own. This is the primary reason why millions of baby girls were abandoned or outright disposed of during the "One-child" policy era in China. I know this personally, because I spent time in China and adopted one of those girls. China's current birth rate? 1.18 in 2022.

Ooops. China's in trouble.

Pivoting to the US, if you're wondering why, it's so difficult to find reliable, responsive, cost-effective tradesman any more, it's because they just aren't there in the number they used to be. **There's a massive demographic shift happening in the US workforce**.

The US birth rate was 1.68 in 2020. *Ruh-roh Raggy* (That means "oh sh!t" if you're not a Scooby Doo fan).

Are you aware that the current replacement ratio of carpenters is 1:8? That means for every eight retiring, there is one replacement. I know the math, because one of my companies is a #1 contractor with the Union of Carpenters and Joiners of America. Doug McCarron and his team have built one of the finest, most resilient trade unions in the world. The ratio is similar in the other construction trades. In fact, when it comes to professions like accounting, it's more like 1:10 for CPAs/Bookkeepers and even worse in old-tech and healthcare!

Any young high school graduate with good guidance and mentoring to encourage them to consider the trades right now, can set themselves up for a lifelong, well-paying career in as little at 18 months! I have my opinions on the value of "education" in Universities and Colleges, but the books, statistics, and my comments throughout this book speak for themselves. With the demographic and energy data you've seen, it starts to make some sense when you look at the mad rush to build AI data centers around the world doesn't it? I elaborate on this in a future chapter on technology. Americans and other developed nations are going to have to figure out how to work again and compete in regional marketplaces. *That is of course if we don't blow ourselves up first.*

RESILIENT PATH INSIGHT: If you're a parent with high-school aged children, are you aware that the fastest growing education sector in my region of the country are trade schools? Local businesses are financially sponsoring and supporting trade schools* to provide trained, ready-to-work employees right out of high school. With an average pay scale of more than 40K and no college debt, it must be a serious consideration. Most youth I know who are doing this are setting themselves up for a lifetime occupation and opportunities to be their own bosses in as little as 18 months.

We are going to very quickly move into a "less technical" society over the next decade. Before you scoff, here's why: *Robots and AI only get you so far.* We are not at a point where we have a next-generation energy-system with ample, excess energy, let alone the raw materials to automate everything. This leaves us with human labor and supplemental technology for our most important tasks. Automation and AI will have their places in manufacturing, logistics, transportation, legal documentation, retail shopping, military, general business services and more, but in very select geographies. As we do figure out how to work again, here are my recommendations for essential tools to have in a rural household. I personally prefer the Milwaukee brand for power tools, but any quality, reliable brand will do!

- 1/2" Electric Impact Wrench* and set of deep well impact sockets* (FWIW, this impact is one of the most valuable tools I've ever used! Used for changing tires, removing/installing large bolts & nuts are a breeze.)

- Cordless tools—all the basics including a hex driver, drill, Skilsaw, Sawzall, etc.

- LOTS of shovels, round and square

- Spade

- Pickaxe

- Wood splitting axe, wedges and maul

- Basic hand tools like screwdrivers, end wrenches and socket wrenches

- Wood hand saw

- 5 and 10 lb. sledgehammers

- Voltage and continuity tester

- Lots of high-quality duct tape (of course)—Gorilla is my favorite brand

- Stihl or Husqvarna chainsaw with a 12–18" Bar

> **RESILIENT PATH INSIGHT:** Cordless batteries—As much as you can invest in batteries and chargers for your cordless tools, do it! Batteries are expensive, and having spares is the name of the game. However, you will eventually need to find someone who has a reliable supply of replacement lithium battery cells to get your cells replaced over time.

Eventually your batteries will not recharge. If you're using your batteries regularly, they will likely all fail in a short span of time! If you're stocking up on replacement cells for a later date, make absolutely sure you're storing them safely, at the optimal charge level* and in proper containers! Lithium batteries require particular care and handling when replacing them in battery packs, so whoever does it, must do it in a reliable, consistent manner similar to original manufacturer specifications. Not doing so can lead to the lithium cells overheating, causing a fire or explosive condition!

> **BE RESILIENT TIP:** If you have enough spare batteries, allow your lithium-based power tool batteries to cool before recharging them. It will in some cases DOUBLE the useful life of them! Get out of the habit of charging warm batteries immediately after you drain them!

Chainsaws

Make sure you save plenty of used engine oil or other inexpensive motor oil for chainsaw bar oil—it works just fine! Have several quarts of 2 cycle oil and know how to efficiently and safely mix 40:1 and 50:1 ratios of gas/oil mixed gas. Have several spare chains for your chainsaw and at least one spare bar and spark plug for each chainsaw you own. Manual, round file sharpening is still one of the most simple and effective ways to sharpen your chains. Keep them out of the dirt! Don't over-rev the chainsaw and let the chain dig in the "sweet spot" speed when cutting, you'll get so much more life out of the blade and bar without overheating it! Avoid over-revving the saw if you can help it. It wouldn't be a bad idea to have some spare parts for the pull cord and fuel components as well, such as these Stihl saw pull starter cams and fuel primer bulb:

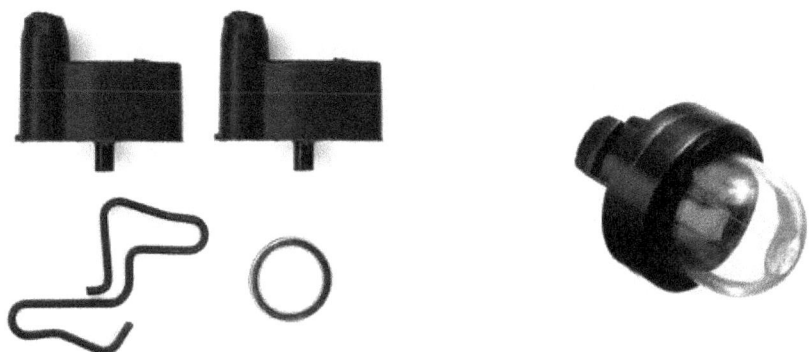

The fuel bulb can dry out and crack/leak, giving you no ability to prime the saw or tool!

Hand Tools

Chainsaw sharpening tool, chainsaw spark plug/chain tensioning tool, Carpenters hand saw, Carpenter's hammer, medium size ball peen hammer, large hitch-mounted or bench-mounted vice, heavy duty punch set, 3/8" ratchet, 1/2" ratchet, 3/8" & 1/2" shallow and deep well socket sets in ANSI AND Metric sizes. 3/8 & 1/2" socket extensions, full set of micro through full size Regular and Phillips screwdrivers. Be sure you have square, hex and allen-style screwdrivers and/or sockets as well. A square shovel, standard rounded shovel, spade, pickaxe, 5 LB sledgehammer, 10 LB sledgehammer, axe, wood-splitting wedges, splitting maul and sharp saw for cutting trees/limbs will all be needed at some point. Quantity one of each, minimum. Buy them as you need them or if you have the extra $$$, buy a full set. All of these are readily available and decent quality and cost at Harbor Freight or for a higher cost at your big box stores. Harbor Freight has a reliable warranty program on their hand tools which is something to consider nowadays.

> **PRODUCT RECOMMENDATION:** By way of a friend's recommendation, I admire the recent innovations by a company called "Toolant." They're reasonably priced and user friendly! Check out the links I've included in the hyperlink reference to see examples of their hex driver socket set*, hex driver allen set*, and allen wrenches*.

Automotive-specific Tools

Acquire oil filter wrenches for your automobiles and heavy equipment filters as well as any "specialty" wrenches if needed for a given piece of equipment. Gear puller set, pulley puller set, harmonic balancer puller, ball joint tool, and tie rod tool are great basics to have.

> **PRODUCT RECOMMENDATION:** This one thing has proven invaluable when servicing engine oil: Fumoto Drain Valves*.

11 - BEYOND THE TESLA FANTASY: CONFRONTING AMERICA'S TRUE ENERGY FUTURE

E lectricity: the bane of modern human existence! Where do I start. Oh, yeah—you can't effectively function in "developed" society without it! Your water supply, hot water, cooking, refrigeration, freezers, food production, food distribution, education system, waste water treatment, daily transportation and employment all depend on it (there are a few minor exceptions).

Think about this for a second: everything in your life is powered by electricity. *If you don't have it for an extended period of time, you have a problem.* A potentially life-altering problem if the outage is longer than a few weeks. We live in an electric society, so much so, electric cars are being promoted as the replacement for combustion engine cars. **Mark my words...I've been saying for years, the current electric car phase is 100% unsustainable and the Tesla is the**

modern-day version of the Delorian. In the Prologue, I covered just one of the main data points showing that electric vehicles aren't the future. Don't get me wrong, I love the Tesla model S in terms of an in-car driving/passenger experience, but not as a resilient, sustainable solution. *Electric cars will be around, but not as a car for a majority of people in currently car-centric societies.*

Yeah, I know hydrogen cars are here and also making a big splash, but to be blunt, it's just another unsustainable, profiteering scam. It will have its place since it has backing of major engine manufacturers such as Toyota and Cummins, but the jury is still out. Based on the data I have; I highly doubt it will replace petroleum-powered autos for the average consumer. Remember my "Cuba car*" comment in the chapter on Transportation and Heavy Equipment? So, what's going to happen?

I keep a close pulse on the energy industry and I can say that from what I'm seeing, we are going to have a major push for the re-start of nuclear power plants to supply power to all the new AI Data Centers being built, but I'm not confident that's going to happen soon enough. This means those Data centers are going to be consuming existing power in the grid which would otherwise be used to maintain reliable service to other industries and residential needs. It won't happen consistently across America tomorrow, *but I'm lowering my expectations on reliability of grid power in the future.*

Other than that, the vast majority of demand-to-be-serviced belongs to natural gas, small nuclear, and Appalachian-coal-fired power plants. From where I'm sitting, those power sources have the greatest potential to be the bridge that gets us to what's next. Next are legitimate, high-efficiency alternatives that can operate at commercial scale through either distributed micro-grids or enhanced centralized systems. **I've seen these alternative solutions with my own eyes and know they exist**.

In the meantime, the investments have been made, and as we move out of the "green energy" and electric vehicle "fad," conventional power generation solutions will begin to make a big resurgence. Here's a map of our complex power generation sources nationwide in the US:

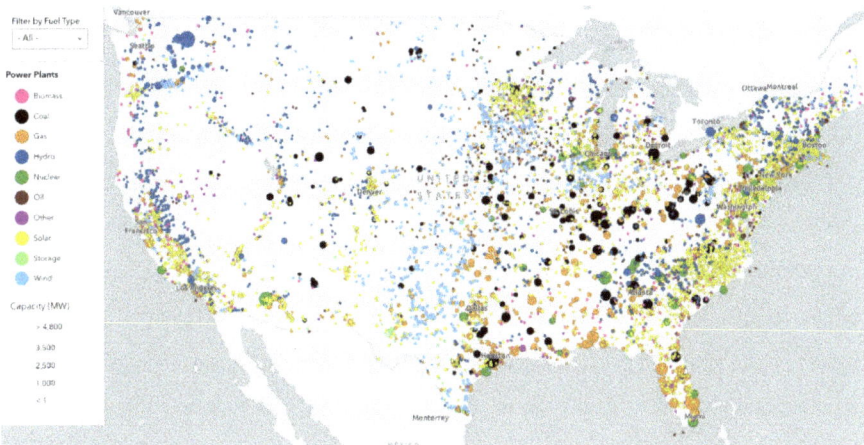

Map as of 2023, Interactive map compliments of Synapse Energy Economics Inc.*

The future of vehicle power is likely going to move to some form of simple "electro-motive" system, smaller versions of the power plant* used in our modern-day train locomotives: a diesel engine and generator combination which creates electricity to turn electric motors which turn the wheels. **It is the most efficient power source for transportation over land (proven for decades in the rail industry)**. This makes a lot of sense when looking at how much diesel fuel and diesel-fuel-infrastructure is used worldwide, coupled with the fact that simple, electric drive systems are highly efficient and make a lot of sense for what's "next." Think of it as the "best of both worlds" when it comes to the use of a petroleum/electric power solution to maintain our over-the-road transportation needs.

The current economics problem inhibiting the widespread development, adoption and retrofitting of cars and trucks in the USA with electro-motive power is our "road tax" structure. *Introducing any of these high-mileage transportation systems crushes road tax revenues*. This plus the fact that the existing energy and other car-related monopolies won't allow this because consumption in the US would rapidly decrease over time. It's a non-starter for them. **Our current complex systems will break if this doesn't change**.

Gasoline

Did you know that the quality of US gasoline has been seriously declining for the last decade? Current gasoline stocks in the US have been shifting from the old traditional sources of Alaska, Gulf of Mexico, Saudi Arabia, North Sea and Russia to a greater dependence on light oils from shale fracking ("Tight Oil" from the graphic in the prior chapter). Two consequences of this are; less energy density of the oil and basic incompatibility with US refineries (which is why we export so much of our shale oil production). Because of this, the gasoline you get from a gas station has a shorter shelf life, so much so, it starts to rapidly lose its "freshness" in as little as 3 MONTHS without treatment. If you treat it with Stabil, you could get as much as 9–12 months of storage, but that is pushing it for reliability.

> **RESILIENT PATH INSIGHT:** Keep enough gas around to run your basics for a short period of time, but focus on other fuel types for the long haul.

As of 2022, roughly 40% of transportation in the US is powered by gasoline, with the vast majority of that being automobiles. There will be plenty of them around for a long time, just know that fresh gasoline is likely going to be an issue in the long-term and become a highly-valued commodity!

Diesel Fuel (aka "Fuel Oil")

Upwards of 40% of global on-road transportation is powered by diesel fuel. Approximately 80%–85% of marine transport is powered by diesel fuel. Approximately 85–90% of global rail transportation is powered by diesel fuel. If you think pure-electric drive systems are going to replace these systems anytime soon in any meaningful way, *you're mistaken*. Diesel is here to stay for a long time, so you can count on it being generally available more so than anything else. Trouble is, the diesel fuel stocks have been suffering from a similar issue as gasoline in terms of quality. #2 is most common in all mild to warmer climates, with #1 being mixed in for use in colder climates due to its thinner consistency, higher burn temperature and lower gelling point.

Have you ever seen several diesel trucks pulled over on the side of the highway when extreme sub-zero temperatures happen in the Midwest? *It's because they didn't have a #1/#2 mix or enough anti-gelling treatment in their fuel.* Diesel fuel at extremely cold temps gels up and stops flowing! You might see this more on the uphill side of a mountain because the engine requires more fuel and power to haul the load up the mountain. More fuel movement through the cold fuel system = faster gelling and stopping of the engine! Modern fuel systems today are better than years past, but still can have gelling issues in extreme weather.

Where's your blind spot?

Here's an example of "subrogation" I mentioned in Chapter 01:

Picture a gas station with a diesel truck filling up at a diesel pump. Every time the truck driver fills up at the pump, there's already tax baked into that price per gallon of fuel. Like buying a toy that comes with batteries included. This is the federal excise tax (about 24 cents per gallon) plus whatever your state adds on top (varies wildly, but usually another 20–50 cents). Now here's where it gets interesting for our world: *this is pure subrogation theater.* The driver pays the tax, but has zero say in how it gets spent. It goes into the Highway Trust Fund, which is essentially a government slush fund that's supposed to fix roads but often gets raided for other projects. The structure is designed to make compliance automatic and invisible. No choice, no jurisdiction, no real contract. Just extraction embedded in the transaction. Classic example of how conventional systems bypass individual sovranty through systemic design. For someone operating a diesel vehicle in our system—say, transporting generators or hauling building materials, we're funding a system we have no control over, for infrastructure we may barely or never use, with no recourse if the funds are mis-allocated. Pure subrogation disguised as "user fees."

Gasoline Storage

My personal favorite is the old steel military "Jerry Can," but they* are in HIGH demand and more difficult to find these days with all the crazy regulations for dispensing fuel. For gasoline, use green or red color gas cans. If you cannot get the "Jerry Cans," then I recommend these*. Never store gasoline cans indoors! Where possible, store them outdoors in a dry place out of the sun. *Never use gasoline as fuel for a fire. If you're lucky enough to have just some burnt eyebrows, burnt body hair and a shock wave big enough to wake your family up (from the house windows shaking), you'll understand why*!

Diesel Storage

If you have and use diesel equipment, have several 5-gallon yellow Jerry Cans for diesel fuel (filled with #2 diesel fuel). If you cannot get the yellow Jerry Cans, these* come in yellow as well. Also store them outdoors in a dry place out of the sun. Diesel has a far-lower flash point than gasoline, so it's a bit safer, but always treat it with respect and *never use it as fuel for a fire*! Most other gasoline and diesel containers have dispensing systems that are just downright AWFUL, so be discrete with what you buy. The blue colored version of these* are used for storing kerosene*. Always keep several plastic funnels handy and keep them clean of dirt and debris.

Gasoline and Diesel Fuel Treatment

It serves two primary functions: Keeps water-in-fuel issues to a minimum and helps keep carburetors in small engines from getting all gunk'd up from sitting for long periods of time! Ethanol in gasoline is a huge problem for small gas engines and gas fuel systems long-term! Keep a few cans of fuel treatment around and add the appropriate dose in the fuel tanks of all your equipment when putting fuel in them. You'll understand why in the long haul!

PRODUCT RECOMMENDATION: Thank God for Seafoam*! It has been a staple in our family for decades and continues to prove its usefulness in keeping gasoline and diesel fuel systems in good working order.

Fuel Stabilizer

Stabil* *is another must have if you're going to store any kind of fuel for an extended period of time.* With all I've shared above when it comes to fuel quality, Stabil will help extend fuel life to justify the extra expense when used correctly. With gasoline, you must keep using it and refreshing what you have on a constant basis without the use of Stabil. *Diesel's a bit better, but still has issues long-term.*

BE RESILIENT TIP: There are different Stabil products for gasoline and diesel, so make sure you're using the right one.

Propane

If there was ever a "perfect" fuel for most of your needs, it would be propane! It's not flawless and requires careful handling of tanks, can be expensive and also difficult to get at times, *but it stores forever.* If I had my way, all of my generators and gasoline engines would be propane-powered, but it's just not realistic. I highly recommend all of your essential systems like backup-generators, water heat and cooking needs be powered by propane.

> **RESILIENT PATH INSIGHT:** When you do decide to use propane for a household (appliances, generator, etc.), buy the biggest tank you can afford and afford to fill! Bury it if at all possible and make sure whoever is burying it knows what they are doing!

Everything fuel and electricity being what it is, the bigger concern I have is the fact that much of our "base load" power generation from nuclear and coal-fired power plants has been decommissioned or is in the process of being decommissioned.

Half of Peak Coal-Fired Generation Capacity to Close in U.S. by 2026

The peak of coal's power generation capacity was in 2011, at 317.6 GW. Just 15 years later, in 2026, half of that capacity will be gone — replaced by gas, wind and utility-scale solar.

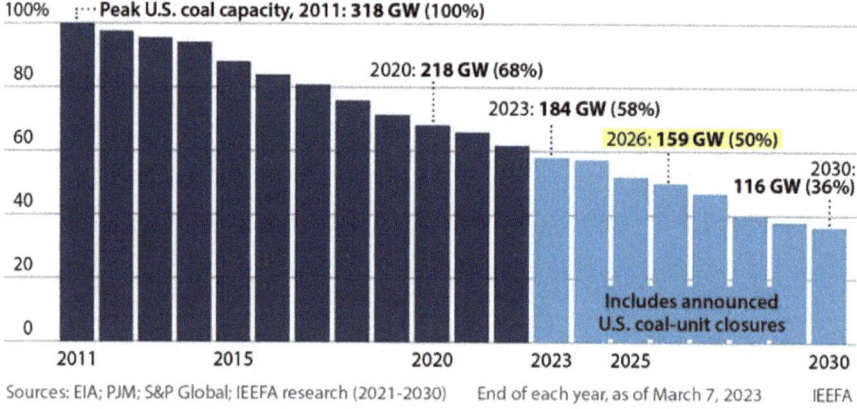

Sources: EIA; PJM; S&P Global; IEEFA research (2021-2030)   End of each year, as of March 7, 2023   IEEFA

This graph shows what decommissioning our coal-fired power production capacity looks like so far.

Here's the link to nuclear reactors already decommissioned*—*all 42 of them.*

Let's talk about foundation: For the last 100 years, our country's power generation was built on coal-fired power plants. We'll have decommissioned 50% of these plants by 2026. We've offset less than 5% of our power grid with 'renewables.' Not sure what the creator of this chart was smoking when he came up with the "replaced by gas, wind and utility-scale solar" part of the caption.

Where's the real gap in power going to come from?

Natural gas-fired plants have taken up some of the slack, which is comical since we've been sold the new power generation sources replacing these coal plants were "green." I'm 100% confident in the math that an equivalent amount of natural gas-fired plants **have not been commissioned to replace the coal** (NIMBY* and the permitting process for a new plant is onerous as it is). To just maintain a quality of life, we must increase our level of resiliency to this obvious reduction in power availability and reliability across the US in the coming years. This is one key area where your resiliency efforts will pay off!

As of this writing, there is a mad rush to build massive, power-gorging Data Centers across the country. Why? There's much speculation, but the fact of the matter is that they're being built and fast-tracked for a reason. My experience and the data tell me there's an effort to massively scale AI due to:

- a developing labor availability crisis

- a need to correlate existing data which has been collected over the last few decades

- command and control infrastructure required for the "Robot Army" I mention in other chapters.

The "correlation of data" is the use of AI for pattern recognition of the product purchase data and Geo-location data from our phones and computers over the last few decades—to build a "social profile" on all Americans.

I cover this in much more detail in the chapters on technology and security.

RESILIENT PATH INSIGHT: Consider putting yourself in a position where you can provide sufficient energy for your household in the long-term. Your access to energy is directly proportional to your quality of life!

12 - THE TRIBALISM RETURN: PREPARING FOR CONFLICTS MOST AMERICANS REFUSE TO SEE COMING

This chapter is oriented towards Americans, but wherever in the world you have remaining freedoms to own and operate firearms, this applies to you! *Whatever you do, keep personal defense simple.*

The best defense is simply just being prepared and resilient. It puts you on a solid footing so you can effectively respond to circumstances, instead of being at the mercy of others. **Ignore this at your own peril**.

Firearms

There's a reason the right to firearms ownership is the 2nd Amendment to the US Constitution and not the 10th! I have a feeling most Brits, Canadians, Australians, New Zealanders or South Africans would tell you it was a mistake to allow themselves to be effectively disarmed with the firearms restrictions implemented in those countries in recent history. *For those of you who romanticize about being in a gunfight, consider alternative paths before exchanging gunfire!* The statistics are high enough that there's a good chance you'll be mortally wounded in a gunfight and you're done (dead), leaving those who depend on you in a real predicament. **Avoid an armed conflict if at all possible.**

It doesn't mean you're a coward. It's sometimes necessary for self-defense, just be smart and don't go looking for trouble. You're much more valuable alive and able-bodied to yourself, family, and as an American than a statistic. The go-to choices for personal resiliency and self-defense weapons are simple in my book:

- One .22 semi-automatic pistol

- One .22 rifle, preferably semi-automatic like the Ruger 10/22

- 9mm handgun for each adult (whatever is most comfortable for you to shoot)

- 9mm machine pistol with red dot sight for each adult

- 12GA Shotgun for each adult

- One .223 Rifle with scope or red dot sight (AR15 or Mini14)

- Two .308 Rifles, one bolt action with scope and one semi-auto with iron sights or other optics for effective shooting 50-200 yards

If you're brand new to firearms, start with the .22 and work your way down the list. **Safety first always, store in a secure, but accessible location, and practice, practice, practice.** Get comfortable with each firearm you own to the point where you can load it and operate it safely, *blindfolded or in the dark.* **Never ever let a child or other person without gun safety knowledge or unstable mental capacity handle a firearm**! I know so many families and friends who don't practice! You must practice! Get together with family and friends on a regular basis. Make shooting practice a regular event! Just do it! It's an obligation as Americans if we are to continue the American Dream. We often get caught up and are so distracted with daily obligations, we lose sight of this fact: *hundreds of thousands of our fellow Americans fought and died to preserve this and other freedoms we still have.* **Be grateful, and respect their sacrifice!**

BE RESILIENT TIPS: Have at least 500 rounds for each firearm you own. Just be consistent with what you buy, buy quality and buy what works best in each weapon. For the 12GA Shotgun, make sure you have an ammo mix of about 60% bird shot, 30% 00 buckshot and 10% rifled slugs. The bird shot will not only be used for shooting game birds to eat, but also downing drones and other tools used by our adversaries. The buckshot is for general defense. The slugs are for projecting force for defense and big game to eat. Acquire (and load) at least 4–5 spare magazines for each 22, 9mm and rifle. Depending on your state and city, state and local gun laws will dictate how large the magazines can be. I'm sure debate will come up about my recommendations, so here's some further context:

BE RESILIENT TIPS (CONT'D):

- The .22 rimfire is the most widely used and recognized cartridge in the world

- 9mm is the standard for most USA law enforcement agencies and is widely available

- .223 (5.56mm*) is the NATO standard and widely produced/available. NOTE: .223 and 5.56mm are not simply interchangeable, make sure your rifle is designed to safely fire both cartridges with frequent use

- .308 is a variant of the 7.62mm* family of cartridges, is slightly larger than the others, more powerful and also widely produced/available

- 12GA shotgun shells* are the most common in the world

My recommendations here are what they are...recommendations. They're based on my decades of experience and research (I've been an avid hunter since the age of 8). If you have an investment in a firearm that falls outside of these recommendations and you can shoot it well, great. Just make sure you have plenty of ammo. If you run out, I'm sure there will be other alternatives to turn to when the time comes!

RESILIENT PATH INSIGHT: For what it's worth, I love the .44 magnum - powerful, versatile, and extremely accurate for a pistol cartridge. There are also options out there to buy rifles* chambered in .44 magnum. Anytime you like a particular pistol cartridge and you can have a rifle chambered in the same, do it! .22, 9mm, .357, .44 are just some examples.

Optics (scopes, red dots, iron sights, etc.)

> **PRODUCT RECOMMENDATION:** My favorite and recommended optics provider is by far Vortex Optics*. They make great gear. The reason they are #1 on my list is their customer service. You will not find better support and service in the firearms industry!

For any scope requirements, just a simple, rugged, reliable scope will do. One that will perform up to a couple hundred yards. If you have the opportunity to have your optics professionally sighted-in by a reputable gunsmith, it's worth spending the money.

Red dot sights are great for most other firearms. Again, keep it simple and reliable.

> **BE RESILIENT TIP:** My personal favorite for firearms is iron sights. They're resilient, work in the worst of conditions and are old school effective! They do require near 20/20 vision and some practice to use effectively, but you can't go wrong with them. Other than snipers and very few other specialized units, in WW2, the standard was iron sights!

I could elaborate further on the merits of various barrel materials & types, blued-steel vs. parkerizing vs. cerakote vs. stainless, nickel-boron bolt carrier groups (BCGs), triggers, handgun slides, flash suppressors, rifle gas systems and much more, but those are incremental benefits and fine tuning typically for shooters with significant experience and pocketbooks!

Knives

There are soooooo many options and varieties, I simply have a few recommendations. Own a set of "dressing" knives like this*. I have practical experience with this set and they work well! If you're going to acquire knives, acquire knives that will last a lifetime.

There's nothing better than a practical, sharp knife. This one from Dawson Knives*
is one of the finest I've ever owned.

My years as a commercial fisherman taught me precision with a blade. I've processed tens of thousands of fish and dressed countless game animals. When your livelihood depends on clean, efficient knife work, you develop skills that extend far beyond the dock. There is no substitute for a razor-sharp, good quality, comfortable-to-use knife! You would never know it, but the knife above is outstanding for filleting and preparing fish for the grill or storage! Keep a good knife accessible as much as you can, but be mindful to take it out of your bag before going through security screening at an airport or other places!

Bows

If you have or can acquire and get skilled at the use of a bow and arrow, it's a serious asset. Quiet and more effective than bullets in certain cases, they are very under-rated! I love crossbows. A good one nowadays can be purchased and outfitted well for just a few hundred bucks! No limitations here like firearms in terms of ownership, so the sky's the limit... There are restrictions in terms of

128

where/when you can hunt using crossbows and archery equipment, so do your due diligence and learn local, state and any federal laws.

Fire

Your worst enemy bar none.

> **PRODUCT RECOMMENDATION:** For defense against typical fires, have one or more large Carbon Dioxide fire extinguishers* available at your home or homestead and a small one in the kitchen—NOT ABC chemical fire extinguishers.

The fact of the matter is that the contents of an ABC fire extinguisher are toxic and corrosive and render everything you spray it on unusable and requires time-consuming, expensive cleanup, especially in kitchen or eating areas!

There are four classes of fires, but the three most common types of fires are Class A, B and C:

- Class A is a fire fueled by solid combustibles like wood, paper, cardboard, etc. (like a campfire)

- Class B is a fire fueled by liquid combustibles like grease, oil, gasoline, etc. (like a stovetop grease fire)

- Class C is an electrical fire caused by overloads, bad wiring, or component failure. Example: a corroded plug connection overheats and ignites the wire casing.

You can effectively use a carbon dioxide fire extinguisher on any Class B or Class C fire.

Water is your best bet for putting out a Class A fire, but be careful. If you try to put out a house fire with water and the main electrical panel is not shut off, you could electrocute yourself and/or others!

> **RESILIENT PATH INSIGHT:** As a young child, I watched my father run to a neighbor's house and traverse a 4' fence on the run with a 20 LB carbon dioxide fire extinguisher in hand to put out a fire inside their house when they weren't home. He put the fire out long enough for the fire department to get there in time to save the house from being burned to the ground!

I've used carbon dioxide extinguishers many times in my life. Here's the most important things to know:

- They're easy to use—and work very well at depriving a fire of oxygen

- A carbon dioxide fire extinguisher is your best friend for dealing with just about any fire you experience in your life!

- They are safe to use on electrical equipment that is live and energized

- They don't make a mess when you use them!

- Do not spray anyone or any part of something that can be burned from the extreme cold of the CO2 vapor—*that is of course unless someone is on fire*!

- Carbon dioxide extinguishers will not be as effective on a Class A fire, but can be used to slow it down until you can get water on it!

RESILIENT PATH INSIGHT: *There is no effective way to extinguish a lithium battery fire with any type of fire extinguisher.* Once they start burning, they are self-feeding and the only way they stop is when the fire burns through all of the fuel in the battery chemistry. This is why having lithium batteries in a proper fire-safe container during recharging is essential.

The real reason for details on fire is this—we are moving into a time where "tribalism" is going to come back with a vengeance.

Yes, I'm talking "Cowboys and Indians" type tribalism.

You can already see our country fracturing, and I expect this will only increase should the current trends be allowed to continue. We do have a choice: do something about it or not. If not, be prepared for the consequences which include something as serious as losing the unity of our current 50 states and life-changing impacts to you and your family.

Fire defense must be an absolute priority.

Exterior surfaces on homes are best if covered with non-combustible materials like brick, steel siding or steel roof. All those asphalt shingle roofs you see in subdivisions across the country—*have an unrefined version of oil on their roof and are highly combustible.* These aren't the worst. How about wood shake shingles? A homeowner's and insurance underwriter's worst nightmare.

RESILIENT PATH INSIGHT: Be continually aware of situations inside and outside your household or other buildings which could cause a fire; solvent-saturated rags in garbage cans, unsupervised trash pile burning on a windy day, bad or loose electrical wiring, overloaded power cords, combustible fabrics near open flame, corroded RV power cord connectors, etc.

As tribalism increases, the fact that millions of homes across the country have vinyl or wood siding is going to be a major issue in the future. The fires in California and Lahaina Hawaii are recent examples that come to mind of what can happen when fires get out of control. In these two cases due to natural and man-made causes.

You may remember my comment about fire in a prior chapter on "shelter" and what an antagonist can do to get you to move?

<u>Close Combat</u>

99.9% of people are not prepared for close combat! I personally learned some painful lessons at a young age and learned how to effectively defend myself. The best and simplest approach is stated by the character Dalton from the 80's classic *Roadhouse*: "Nobody ever wins a fight."

Always do what you can to avoid conflict—and don't forget why the First Amendment to the Constitution is the first (speech vs. force).

However, if you are forced to fight:

- Fight like your life depends on it, because it just might

- No rules, just do what's necessary to survive

- FAST outcomes are best (like within the first 10 seconds fast!)

- If you're going to invest time and effort into improving your resiliency for close combat, focus on disciplines proven in competitive environments: Brazilian Jiu-Jitsu, boxing, Muay Thai, or wrestling.

If you're thinking it might be a good idea to get in better physical condition based on what I just shared and to improve your personal resiliency overall, *that would be wise.*

13 - VALUE WITHOUT DOLLARS: THE COMING RENAISSANCE OF SKILLS-BASED EXCHANGE

I f you didn't read the Prologue, *now would be a good time to do so*. Barter and exchange are a natural part of the "Pause. Prepare. Participate." process. Participate—it's literally what makes a society what it is.

It's our intentional interaction with others in the proper Capacities, Jurisdictions and Contracts—ideally creating value for all parties involved. Extreme mis-alignments and blind spots in this process create imbalances of value, which lead to conflict, disruption and resets (divorce is one example). Knowing how to confidently Pause. Prepare. Participate. in barter and exchange is essential to be resilient. Barter and exchange are truly a lost art in America. *But making a comeback.*

With inflation continuing to increase and availability of skilled tradesman decreasing rapidly, you're going to have to learn how to barter and exchange. Inflation is a currency phenomenon: the outcome when a currency is mismanaged by governments (such as the US Dollar), allowing excessive debt, fraud and speculation. We have ZERO real control over inflation of the US Dollar, but do have the ability to transact in different "currencies" such as barter and exchange.

Skills

Your first, best, barter-able asset. Depending on your age, you've probably gained some meaningful experience in a few professions or hobbies. Double and triple-down on honing these skills if you enjoy them, especially if they are skills that have strong current demand. If you don't have skills which are in demand, find something you enjoy doing which people need and invest time and energy there. It's quite simple, don't over-complicate it. Just make a decision and do it. Better just to get started and be consistent than not start at all.

PRODUCT RECOMMENDATION: For all you entrepreneurs out there, here's my first mention of the book The Right It*—mandatory reading for new AND experienced entrepreneurs!

Eggs

As you probably guessed from my prior recommendation in the chapter on food, one of my top recommendations for bartering is raising egg-laying chickens to produce fresh chicken eggs. They are relatively easy to raise, inexpensive and enjoyable to have around! People have to eat, and as you've read in prior chapters on health and food preparation, you understand the importance of having nutrition-dense food and a high-value source of protein. I expect egg prices in the supermarket to continue to rise exponentially in the coming years. *Millions of chickens were culled in the recent past to "prevent" another pandemic. Have you heard of it? BIRD FLU**. Guess which bird is being blamed—**chickens**. If you have enough chickens to produce eggs for your family, great—protect them at all costs! You literally won't be able to afford to lose them. The good news is, it doesn't take much to add a few more chickens to your flock and boost your daily production. You'll find this is going to prove quite valuable to your household in the future and is a wise investment if you're able to do it!

Food (in general)

Canned, freeze-dried, packaged or fresh food is an invaluable asset and you'll find ways to barter with it when the time comes. You lose nothing by growing, preparing and storing food: either you will consume it in the future when needed or use it for barter. Simply having it in your possession is what counts!

Nutritional Supplements

Vitamin D3 and Vitamin C are your staples, with Vitamin K, A, E, Zinc and Calcium next. If you can afford and have the conditioned space indoors for other supplements I've mentioned in prior chapters, then acquire and store what you can. Remember, supplements don't store forever, so buy quality and use/rotate what you have if at all possible.

> **BE RESILIENT TIP:** Choose liquid or gelcap supplements over tablets—they absorb more effectively.

Special Skills or Equipment

In practical terms, the previously covered barter-able items are very useful. However, the fact is that not everyone needs eggs or can even afford to barter for your skills. This is where having a special skill or special equipment comes into play. Something no one in your immediate area has that you can leverage long-term as either a paid-for-service or barter item. For example, I have heavy equipment and a rotary hydraulic driver* attachment from Digga USA. The sandy/silty soils of Coastal GA and N FL in many cases require pilings for the structural support of houses, commercial buildings, decks, piers, solar panel farms, power poles and much more. It's also useful with a special attachment* to auger out tree stumps. Unique hand tools such as a pex expansion tool*, plate steel saw* or others will be invaluable for bartering in the future! If a house gets destroyed or rendered uninhabitable by a hurricane in the future, it's highly likely there's pex tubing and structural steel that can be salvaged and re-used* from the building! *These kinds of tools are required in order to make most efficient use of these reclaimed materials.* These are just a few of dozens of examples. Since barter is a lost art, it will take a while for it to widely catch on in our communities. That's o k. **In the meantime, be planning for it**.

Regardless of what the future holds, you lose nothing by improving your resiliency in these areas. If for no other reason than this: *the robot army is coming*. One thing is clear, a mechanical army of laborers, policemen and soldiers is coming and coming fast (definitely in my lifetime). **The greatest challenge I see with robots is the reshuffling and potential de-rating of human-priorities**. Let me explain: if you're a wealthy billionaire who has a monopoly or near monopoly in a business sector, the greatest challenge ahead of you in the coming years is labor availability and trade restrictions due to the demographic issues I've shared in prior chapters. There's a balancing act they constantly play between cost of labor, import/export tariffs, transportation expense, supply chain logistics, etc. depending on where their business is located. *Robots level this playing field.* If monopolies can build a robot labor workforce in the US and supply goods to consumers in the US without having to deal with increasing labor cost, labor unions or human workforce burden in general (only work 8 hours/day, HR expense, benefits, sick days, major illness, retirement), then they've got the perfect scenario.

Now you know the primary reason behind the recent Longshoreman's strike: fear of automation. The union is concerned and they should be—not because automation's a bad thing, but because *they are unable to adapt fast enough to the changes* and demonstrate their value in other ways (such as robots and robotic management systems, maintenance, institutional knowledge). China and others are already doing it with the shipping container handling in their ports. In the next 10 years, vast job occupations are going to be automated and render human participation in them obsolete. Bad news for labor-intensive jobs, *great news for people who understand this shift* and learn how to become resilient to these changes! There is a mind-boggling number of opportunities which are going to emerge with these changes if you know how to go "where the puck is going to be," much like the famous hockey player Wayne Gretzky* mastered.

Ammo

.22LR is a widely recognizable item to barter with. I recommend investing in a few extra 500 round bricks. Even if you don't have a .22, someone you know has one—and will need the ammo in the future. If you're not familiar with recent events in the world of .22 ammo, they are currently running about 6ish cents per round. There was a time in recent history when one round cost as much as 34 cents! Acquire these and other recommended items as you have available funds, time and effort. Then watch as your improved resiliency pays off! Other cartridges

I mentioned previously are not a bad investment, but everything in moderation and as it makes sense for you and those around you.

Silver

In my experience and research, this is the ultimate means of barter, in particular pre-1965 US silver dimes and quarters. debate has raged in modern times about this one barter topic alone!

RESILIENT PATH INSIGHT: There's going to come a day when the silver price manipulation stops—yes, it does exist. It will be a day remembered in the history books. If you're fortunate enough to be holding some when that happens, your quality of life will be virtually unaffected and if anything, will improve. Setting expectations properly, it's not to be "traded" for short-term gain—that's a fool's errand. It's simply insurance against governments mis-managing currencies*.

Some reading this will scoff...and I understand why, but here's the facts. During a century of the Roman Empire (staring in 211 BC) the Roman Denarius* was used for decades as the primary currency, ultimately being de-monetized and replaced by another currency. Being about the equivalent in size and silver content of a pre-1965 US silver dime, it was used for general commerce, including payment of the Roman soldier of approximately one denarius per day. Much like the US dime, quarter and other coinage, the amount of silver was eventually removed almost in its entirety. In fact, the dimes, nickels and quarters you use today effectively have ZERO silver in them. Conversely, a pre-1965 Roosevelt dime today has a melt value of $2.35! *That's 2,350% of its face value*!

Silver content in historical context matters. At the turn of the century in the early Great Depression years (1929–1932), an American man working a full days' labor would typically get paid 50 cents per day (let's say 5 dimes, the equivalent of about 1/3 of an oz. of silver). Think about what you get paid in a day today: At the time of this writing, on average it's about $190 per day (1,900 dimes). Using just face value, and history as a guide, silver's prospects are bright indeed! **Americans are going to have to figure out how to work collaboratively again and take charge of our currency-for-value system**. Our labor is our currency and we barter/exchange it for the US Dollar currency to purchase things we need from the marketplace. If we don't figure out how to work and take charge of these things, we're going to continue to slowly be marginalized by illegal immigration and AI/robotics.

Want to know one reason why the US border has been wide open for several years in the recent past? *The monopolies need cheap labor for their operations here in the USA*. In China and Mexico, they already have slave labor making iPhones and other goods...they can't get it any cheaper, and with the pressure to onshore jobs to the US and our accelerating demographic problem, something has to give! As a Constitutional Republic using the US Constitution as our guide, we can and should utilize robots in the open market in such a way as to generally increase the quality of life for all Americans—not just monopolies and special interests.

> **BE RESILIENT TIP:** To the younger generations reading this: the world is your oyster if you figure out how to improve your resiliency, work smart and hard with the right mentorship and guidance!

We Americans are at a crossroads as a civilization, and specifically a crossroads in leadership. We have a bunch of wealthy industrialists and finance moguls who have great influence over governments around the world. They've clearly demonstrated they are willing to leave the middle and lower classes behind to continue to amass wealth, power and control. This is why there is so much talk about "Universal Basic Income" (UBI). This is synonymous to Marie Antoinette's disconnectedness with the realities of society and her famous saying "Let them eat cake" (and she ultimately lost her head for it, literally). As I've elaborated earlier, I don't see anyone in US government or businesses realistically addressing or being able to address this issue, not even Elon Musk. This doesn't mean socialism or communism, because those "equitable" systems result in horrific outcomes and have proven many times in history that they don't work.

> **RESILIENT PATH INSIGHT:** If you want a truly grounding experience in reality and a look into one of the worst episodes of what happens when "equitable" systems run amok, look no further than Darryl Cooper's The Anti-humans*—a concise, in-depth exposé of the atrocities which took place during the Bolshevik Revolution in early 1900s Russia. ***CAUTION—READING OR LISTENING TO IT IS NOT FOR THE FAINT OF HEART***

Any solution must have consideration for everyone and everything built into it—where the average person can realize a decent, humane, quality-of-life, being able to mature personally and raise a family in a safe, healthy environment. Wishful thinking, I know—*but someone has to say it and offer up real solutions.* We all have our gifts and abilities. Some of us are destined to be tradesman for the rest of our lives, and that's ok as long as the tradesman (man or woman) has an opportunity to live a decent life which is supported at all levels of our society and governance.

Is it a perfect world? No. Can we do better and utilize these technological advancements to legitimately advance as human beings? Yes, we certainly can. As I demonstrated in the Prologue—dreams of solar panels, wind farms and electric cars are niche solutions at best for the wealthy class. This begs the question...are we being left behind? Ever seen the movie Zardoz*? *Warning: it's a crazy, trippy 70's flick, so be mindful of the viewing audience*! Its plot is something to ponder. Don't worry, in the chapter on Community and Collaboration, I take on this issue and provide you some options with positive outcomes that work for all Americans and people around the world!

14 - ANALOG REVIVAL: RECLAIMING SIMPLE TECHNOLOGIES THAT CAN'T BE HACKED

I've lost a bunch of hair and have a lot of Grey in my beard from the topic of information technology and how it affects us. It's not an easy one to deal with.

We are organic beings. Our bodies were not designed to work well with all of the electronic "noise" around us. In fact, there's a growing body of decades of evidence that shows clearly our over-interaction with digital screens, over-exposure to wireless signals and lack of interaction with nature is slowly degrading our quality of life.

Technology advancements and sophistication have dramatically outpaced

a human's ability to interact with it*! Having spent more than half my life immersed in the most advanced technologies in the world, I can say that we as humans only use a mere fraction of a fraction of a percent of the technical capacity and capabilities which exist—*it's overwhelming*. If you wonder why, you feel like you're overwhelmed, *it's because you are*.

> **BE RESILIENT TIP:** Begin to re-simplify your life as much as possible by moving back to an analog life whenever and wherever practical.

Does it mean you have to "give up" technology? No, but improving your resiliency and creating a higher quality of life for yourself does require minimizing or eliminating the bad habits we've developed when using it. Buying a car? *Opt for manual windows, manual door locks and minimal electronics.* **Those "conveniences" make you less resilient and more stressed**. How? Manual door locks and window mechanisms are much less prone to breakage or failure. **Simplicity = Resiliency**. The more complex you make something, the more "vectors" of attack there are! This is a bit off topic, but relevant: did you know that Russia figured out how to defeat Ukrainian electronic warfare drone jamming systems across the battlefield in 2024? How?

Using a fiber-optic tether instead of wireless electronics!

> **BE RESILIENT TIP:** Begin to move back to using wired connections wherever possible.

The future long-term health impacts are still unknown by having Bluetooth earbuds INSIDE the protective perimeter of your skull, *especially our youth*! Use "over-the-ear" headphones such as Bose, Sony, V-Moda, Shure or another reputable brand. If at all possible, use a wired audio connection instead of Bluetooth.

> **RESILIENT PATH INSIGHT:** I don't know about you, but being a brain cancer survivor, I'm placing my bets on wired, over-the-ear headsets being better for my quality of life and longevity vs. wireless. Based on what I've seen and experienced, you should too.

Get a nice, practical phone case like this* to allow you to use a magnet holder to keep your phone at arms-length away from you as much as possible. Keep your phone in your pants pocket to a minimum. *Spending time in close proximity to devices emitting serious electromagnetic energy is not good for your quality of life!* If you'd like to understand how much is being emitted in your household, then get one of these*. You're not going to get it to zero, that's impractical in today's world. Just be conscious of what device gives off what and do your best to minimize your exposure so your *body has time to compensate*. **The more technology you have in your life, the less resilient you are**. This book is intended to show you where opportunities exist to simplify your life and reduce this dependency, increasing your resiliency. As with anything in life, *there must be balance*. The trick is figuring out the right balance in your life to use the conveniences of modern technology which "improve" your quality of life, but avoid depending 100% on it where it makes you vulnerable to disruption.

Here's where this chapter gets interesting. *Unless you're Amish or living in a legitimately off-grid community somewhere, you're likely dependent on some external technology resource for everything in your life.* You're here and reading this to figure out how to move to a more resilient life. This book is to help you fast track this pivot to resiliency. The data and events you see unfolding around you are pretty clear: technology has created an environment where Americans have become overly reliant on it. **With that comes much pain if those who control the technology decide to use it as a "stick instead of a carrot."** Each of our lives is what it is...we can only change so much, so fast—and that's ok. Whenever and wherever you have the opportunity to align yourself with a more resilient lifestyle, do it!

The toughest part for all of us is finding communities where there's like-minded souls with resources—souls intent on: advocating a practical, healthy balance of the use of technology and the natural environment, have off-grid resilient power systems, have an opportunity to grow copious amounts of food and have access to regional economic opportunities. I cover what we're doing to lay the groundwork and new framework for American Rural Resilient Communities in a later chapter. Sadly, I haven't found any viable community options out there, which is partly the reason for this book. We must create our own communities: either where we're at or in a net-new development using a well thought out, balanced approach.

I've created a 90-minute Sovran Community Development working session* to collaborate with serious developers, builders, and community leaders. This is a paid engagement and limited to serious builders with actual capacity and resources: not dreamers hoping someone else will solve their problems.

The brutal truth: You can spend years searching for something that doesn't exist, or 90 minutes learning how to create it.

Limited to serious builders only. If you're ready to stop searching and start creating, this is where your community begins."

15 - BEYOND VPNS AND PASSWORDS: THE SECURITY BLIND SPOTS MOST AMERICANS IGNORE

I'm sure you've seen in movies and TV shows inferences or direct references to your "smart phone" spying on you. *I'll make sure this is perfectly clear—**your smart phone is a surveillance and tracking device that acts as a convenient phone and camera for you**.*

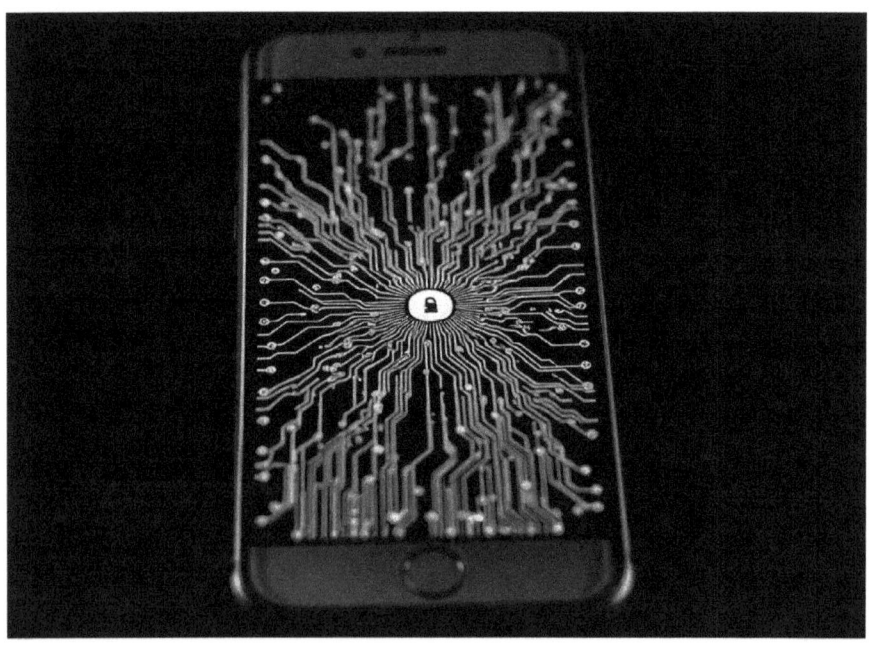

BE RESILIENT TIP: If you'd like the ability to "disappear on demand" from smartphone surveillance, then I recommend acquiring "Go Dark" bags here*. You'll find them in the "Accessories/more accessories" section. Thanks to Greg Hunter at USAWatchdog* for first making me aware of them. They work well and are a great conversation starter! Get at least one for your phone to start and add more bags for devices as you develop a privacy routine.

It's incredibly difficult to disconnect from our social media, messaging apps, email and other notifications. After you try it, you'll find much peace and satisfaction knowing you can truly "unplug!" Getting re-connected with our environment and nature is going to take on a whole new meaning and value in our lives. I recommend trying it during a weekend getaway or other activities that take you away from your regular work or personal routines.

BE RESILIENT TIP: The faraday bags isolate the device in them—not the other devices around you. Having yours in a bag when you require privacy is definitely a step in the right direction but know that other devices around you are still collecting information! Buy an extra phone or laptop bag and have it with you to begin to share your experience and benefits of privacy with others! The more you embrace the conveniences of your "smart devices," *the tighter you set that shackle around your ankle which is tethered to a chain and taskmaster.* But, but David...I use it for everything in my life! Exactly, and that's by design. So let me help you with some tips on how to improve your resiliency and security when it comes to your "smart" devices.

> **PRODUCT RECOMMENDATION:** The first thing I would do is acquire this* for all of the electronic devices you can. Bitdefender has been solid for me for a decade now. I'm grateful for this since my go-to technology for anti-keylogging went through a re-branding and for various reasons, bankruptcy. The most valuable aspect of it was the anti-keylogging feature for your Microsoft Windows or MacOS computer. If you're going to get hacked, this is one common vector*.

Passwords

Another "vector" you're likely to get hacked through is your passwords. Use a password manager like 1Password, Protonpass or Dashlane. They are proven, reputable, industrial strength secure password managers.

TIME IT TAKES A HACKER TO BRUTE FORCE YOUR PASSWORD IN 2023

Number of Characters	Numbers Only	Lowercase Letters	Upper and Lowercase Letters	Numbers, Upper and Lowercase Letters	Numbers, Upper and Lowercase Letters, Symbols
4	Instantly	Instantly	Instantly	Instantly	Instantly
5	Instantly	Instantly	Instantly	Instantly	Instantly
6	Instantly	Instantly	Instantly	Instantly	Instantly
7	Instantly	Instantly	1 sec	2 secs	4 secs
8	Instantly	Instantly	28 secs	2 mins	5 mins
9	Instantly	3 secs	24 mins	2 hours	6 hours
10	Instantly	1 min	21 hours	5 days	2 weeks
11	Instantly	32 mins	1 month	10 months	3 years
12	1 sec	14 hours	6 years	53 years	226 years
13	5 secs	2 weeks	332 years	3k years	15k years
14	52 secs	1 year	17k years	202k years	1m years
15	9 mins	27 years	808k years	12m years	77m years
16	1 hour	713 years	46m years	779m years	5bn years
17	14 hours	18k years	2bn years	48bn years	380bn years
18	6 days	481k years	126bn years	2tn years	26tn years

HIVE SYSTEMS ⟩ Learn how we made this table at **hivesystems.io/password**

This is one of many password strength graphics you can find online. This one is just two years old and gives you an idea of the absolute compute strength and sophistication hackers have at their disposal when trying to "brute force" cracking a password. Anything in purple or red is no good! Make sure you backup your password vault at least every 3 months by putting a reminder in your calendar to do it. Save your encrypted vault to an offline device like a secure flash drive or encrypted external hard disk drive so you always have a backup to recover from. Each of these solutions uses something called a "Master Password." For all password managers, this is the weak link. If you don't utilize a R0cK$tAr complex and lengthy password for your master password and protect it like your life depended on it, you're setting yourself up for failure!

BE RESILIENT TIP: Make sure your passwords are always 13 characters or more, always unique, use alpha and numeric characters and use a special character if at all possible.

RESILIENT PATH INSIGHT: I value comments and feedback! If there's a particular subject or subjects, you'd like me to provide additional information about (such as passwords and how to remember longer, more complex ones easily!), let me know here*!

Email

Gmail is great, but treat it as 100% insecure. Same goes for Outlook, O365, Yahoo, etc. If you're serious about improving your personal digital security resiliency, you must use a proven, secure email system such as Proton Mail*. Even Proton Mail is not perfect and you can shoot yourself in the foot, so be diligent! **The #1 way you can get hacked is by clicking on a link or opening a document in an email that has malware or a virus**. Before you click anything, make sure you know the source! *If you don't know or can't verify the source, delete the email.* **You're much better off having someone need to re-send you**

something than have your security compromised by ransomware or other malicious software.

Documents

What can I say...it's a Microsoft Office world! But I wouldn't be a resiliency expert if I didn't also have resilient options here too! If you're a Mac user, the Mac apps are great and there are open-source office apps like OpenOffice and LibreOffice. *I've tried them all, and candidly they're a pain in the a$$ when it comes to interoperability.* One I've recently taken to after much research and use is "ONLYOFFICE." There's much hubbub on the internet about certain nefarious connections, but I have yet to see the least bit of instabilities or other issues with it. *A word of caution—I don't have enough hindsight and experience to recommend it.* Your best bet is to get standalone licensing for Microsoft Office on your computer and do your best to configure it and use it in such a way so Microsoft is not siphoning copies of your documents up to their systems. I've done this and am confident it's a good solution, *but it requires advanced setup work and is not perfect.*

Document Storage

Cloud storage providers like Google Drive, Microsoft OneDrive and Apple iCloud should be considered insecure—it's ok to use them, but keep this front of mind and don't shoot yourself in the foot. Dropbox, sync and box are better but not perfect. Solutions like Proton Drive and Egnyte are even better, while still maintaining a great amount of convenience and performance. Others may be decent, but use at your own risk. You have to get fairly technical and inconvenient to improve your document storage security beyond this experience. I've utilized vast numbers of solutions including all of the above plus; cryptomator, IDrive, and IronKey. All of them have their merits, so *use what makes most sense for your situation and technical aptitude.*

<u>Wireless Networks</u>

Treat every public wireless network as suspect and only use them while running a VPN. More and more service providers are blocking the use of VPNs because they want to know who is using their services and where they're using them from. I do not recommend connecting to your banking applications via public Wi-Fi connections without the use of a VPN. For obvious reasons.

> **BE RESILIENT TIP:** If you must access your banking connection and cannot use your VPN, connect using your mobile banking phone app using only the cellular network service on your phone (turn off Wi-Fi). In a pinch, you can hotspot tether to your phone as an alternative—again, just make sure Wi-Fi is turned off on your phone.

<u>Text Messaging</u>

Next to electricity, text messaging is the second bane of our existence and #1 weak link for resiliency in personal communication! More people have been caught red-handed in misgivings that led to divorce, political scandals, business breakups, destroyed friendships, destruction of trust, and caused general mis-communication between human-beings. Human beings are bad communicators naturally, without the technology. No wonder we are so divided!

Apples' iMessage, Google Messages and WhatsApp are ok for general conversation, but do everything you can to develop habits using Signal Messenger* for as much of your general conversations as possible, *most importantly business and other highly personal conversations, pictures and phone calls.* **All other mainstream text messaging apps are suspect and just assume they cannot be trusted**. Like Proton Mail, Signal Messenger will not keep you from shooting yourself in the foot!

BE RESILIENT TIPS:

- Signal Messenger has a feature called "disappearing messages." Set your sensitive conversations to a short "disappearing messages" time-frame to minimize the data sitting on your phone. The best way for an antagonist to get your Signal messages is when they get your unlocked phone! Disappearing Messages takes care of this!

- When calling someone via Signal Messenger, it uses the data network, not the voice network. Since it's encrypting the call real-time, it doesn't do well transitioning between cellular towers and you might lose your connection while driving. Best to be stationary if at all possible while you're using this feature.

The Signal Messenger phone app is much more stable and reliable than the desktop app, so don't be surprised if you lose some messages at some point on your desktop when you have to upgrade the software!

Also, don't be upset if for some reason you're unable to recover messages if you lose your phone…Signal is designed to protect your privacy, so these types of experiences are features and not bugs!

Where's your blind spot?

When the Berlin wall separating East and West Germany fell in late 1989, western intelligence agencies were able to get access to East German Stasi* surveillance records and methods. At that time, East Germany had about 16 million residents. When the surveillance records were recovered, our intelligence agencies *discovered approximately 1 BILLION paper records the Stasi had accumulated.* They knew when their adult residents: slept, worked, went to the bathroom, had coffee with friends, had sex with their spouse, had an affair, kids played together, said subversive things over the phone, met with other subversives, etc. You get the point. *Near total surveillance without technology*. **Where do you think our three letter agencies learned the surveillance methodologies in place today?** This is not speculation. Souls like Julian Assange (who's paid a great price) and Edward Snowden proved and articulated this very clearly. Fast forward to today—*every call, every data bit that's transferred over external networks, every movement is collected and stored.*

By now you've figured out I don't pull any punches—nearly all of the mechanisms for a modern Stasi-like totalitarian state are in place. All it takes is a few more bad actors in the wrong key leadership positions to remove remaining resilient legal protections we have and the average American is toast. Overwhelming? *Absolutely*. Unstoppable or unlivable? *Definitely not!* The US Constitution has proven incredibly resilient against many subversives in our past—**the trouble we are facing is because the US Constitution requires active participation of resilient Americans to maintain it!** We have an obligation to create a prosperous potential future for or country and in particular the quality of life for our children, their children and their children's children!

RESILIENT PATH INSIGHT: Millions of Early American Settlers, American Indians, East German Citizens, Yugoslavians, Soviet Russians, Chinese, North Koreans, Cambodians, Chileans, Cubans and other oppressed citizens throughout history died simply because they were attempting to live peacefully and provide a better life for themselves and their families. Utilize these recommendations and others throughout this book to create an improved level of resiliency in light of these facts of life.

BE RESILIENT TIP: these recommendations are not a "bullet-proof" vest that you put on to protect you from bullets. You can make a mistake and get shot in a place your vest doesn't protect! Don't be afraid, just be more informed, diligent and resilient than everyone else.

The best analogy applying to everything digital security is the analogy of the hunters and the Grizzly bear—*if you happen to surprise or piss off a Grizzly and it comes to attack you, best you run faster than your fellow hunter(s)!* This section is intended to help you clearly see a path in your life for digital security resiliency, but it does require work. *Learn, apply and do consistently what I've shared that makes most sense for your personal situation.*

Communications Security

While we do live in a precarious world, we can for the most part communicate with each other in effective ways to conduct ourselves during peacetime in society. Should this change, be prepared to communicate securely by learning something as basic a Morse code. Not secure you say? Do you know anyone who knows Morse code? I know maybe 2 or 3... That said, there's several non-digital ways to communicate with general privacy:

- Morse code

- Hand written letter

- Fax

- Book cypher

Morse code and the cypher methods require time to learn, and more than one person to know how to operate, but can be quite effective when you know how to use it!

Physical Security

Not much has changed here and keep it simple; good fences, gates, security cameras, strong doors, bump-proof locks*, dog(s), ready-access* to self-defense measures including firearms, and good situational awareness skills are still most effective.

> **RESILIENT PATH INSIGHT:** If you can "see" at night, it creates an exponential tactical advantage in terms of resiliency. Consider night vision equipment—not mickey-mouse sh!t, real night vision like PVS-14 or other proven, military-grade night vision optics.

As I mentioned in a prior chapter, make sure you have a means of protecting yourself and physical property from a drone attack. This is proving to be quite effective in modern warfare and should be taken seriously!

16 - RETURN OF THE PRINT RESISTANCE: WHY PHYSICAL BOOKS ARE YOUR BEST DEFENSE AGAINST AI CENSORSHIP

With what I'm seeing in the world of AI and having immersed myself in the world of "Large Language Models," "Model Training," "Tokens," and "Retrieval Augmented GPTs," here's what I've discovered: AIs are not "artificial" or "intelligent" at all.

They are simply large stores of language data from various sources (including Wikipedia by the way) which have been "trained" to utilize various human communication languages to operate and *compose logic-based responses to questions at lightning speed: it's called a Large Language Model or "LLM" for short.* Some LLM's you may be familiar with: ChatGPT, Claude, Gemini, LlaMA, BERT or Mistral. Open AI dominated the space early, but the AI field has diversified much. Each of these models has a "specialty," which can be computer software program creation, human language translation, highly scalable business functions, and much more.

Behind the scenes, they've been built by humans, trained by humans **and are being censored by humans.** From what I've seen thus-far, in large part, what's happening is an attempted digital-book-burning of biblical proportions. If that doesn't scare the living sh!t out of you, it should. Can AI do good? Most definitely. Is it being used to usher in a world useful to the average person in the world? From what I've seen so far, definitely not.

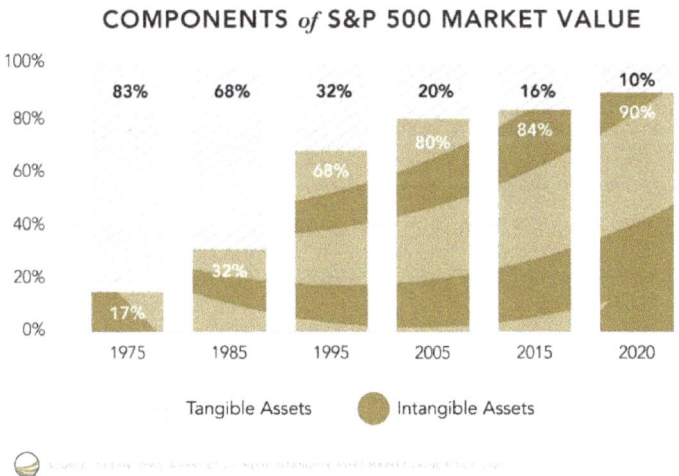

Digital or "intangible" assets make up the vast majority of our world today.

Look who has control of AI: the very tech sector that brought us well-documented and proven censorship during the global pandemic and prior US elections. They are directing the evolution of AI. It takes millions of dollars of compute time, computing resources and investment to develop and train a single large language model like OpenAI's ChatGPT. I'm confident this is an exercise in accelerating the obsolescence of the average person worldwide whenever and wherever possible (hence my reference to UBI in other chapters).

Part of being resilient is not being naive. Educating yourself and knowing if it looks like a duck, walks like a duck and quacks like a duck...it's probably a duck! *What can you do? PLENTY. Start learning everything you can about AI and how it works*—**because everything digital you see is potentially fake**. There's an old saying from a commercial of yesteryear: Is it live or is it Memorex?*. For those of you old enough to understand what that means, it's kind of ironic today. If you don't physically see it for yourself live and interact with a person or person(s) in conversation, *its authenticity is questionable*. Heck, in the near future your phone calls or Zoom calls could potentially have an AI BOT acting as one of your family, friends or business associates! With as much data that's been collected on your face, voice, and your appearance. You can be imitated.

I'm 100% confident this the case. You've seen the deep-fakes of presidential candidates and other spoofs. Don't be naive! Are we at that point yet? No. Is it likely a reality in the near future? *Certainly*. During the first two decades of the 2000's, there's been a cold war going on in the world of data and that war has turned hot.

First, we had "algorithm" changes with Google search engine which completely changed the way search results are returned, often-times with valid data being memory-holed to a point it was nearly impossible to find. YouTube demonetized thousands of highly watched and respected channels, affecting the income of thousands of well-known YouTubers. Twitter (X) and many other platforms changed and people adjusted...moving to Rumble, Substack, Parler and others.

Now, authentic, original data sources are quietly being marginalized, outright censored or forced offline. Websites like archive.org and others which are stores of internet data history are under overt attack*. How long before they are taken offline or "algorithm'd" out of existence? I can clearly see all of the pieces being moved and aligned to "nudge" us to having access to only certain "curated" data sources such as the large language models behind Google's Gemini, Microsoft's CoPilot, and Meta's Meta AI. **Buy physical books...lots of them**. Start your own personal library of books with valuable information such as beekeeping practices, rainwater harvesting, raising chickens, growing food and important historical topics such as the American Revolutionary and Civil Wars.

> **BE RESILIENT TIP:** As you read articles and other sources of valuable information online, save a copy to an offline usb drive or to your local computer. Print it out for your library and make sure that the information is backed-up somewhere secure. A few short years from now you'll understand why!

For those of you who are computer savvy, consider downloading your own AI to your local computer and run your own GPT queries! I like the simplicity of Ollama* and their selection of large language models to choose from. Keep in mind, you must have a computer with some decent compute power, RAM and storage. Some of the models are quite large and can overwhelm your computer. If anything, just try it to learn more about how AI and the data models work. *Have fun with it*! The different results you get from asking the same question to different language models can be quite entertaining! If you have documentation, you've written or accumulated electronically on a particular subject, *did you know you can run an AI Query against it*? That's called a "Retrieval Augmented GPT" or "RAG" for short. Most AI platforms are quickly integrating this feature into their interfaces—It's valuable because it allows you to leverage the power of a large language model with your own data! Retrieval Augmented GPTs are a viable way to utilize the capabilities of AI while preserving data integrity.

Part of being resilient is being honest and demonstrating integrity—respect all copyrighted works and seek permission from authors for anything you haven't authored originally and are considering using publicly! If you don't have permission, do not use it in any way that violates an authors' copyright.

> **BE RESILIENT TIP:** Since essentially everything digital can be manipulated, it's prudent to receive bank, retirement, insurance, brokerage, healthcare and other statements in physical paper form, not digital. If a major bank fails where you have an account and all of their systems are taken offline as the various regulatory agencies and creditors put the pieces together on who's owed what, having physical copies of the past year of your statements is the physical evidence necessary to prove what you had at the time of the event! See the chapter on "Wealth Preservation" for additional steps you can take to protect your wealth. Be sure to keep these important paper records in a fireproof safe or filing cabinet. Don't take my word for it, David Rogers Webb writes extensively about it in his book titled The Great Taking*.

I caution you personally and professionally not to put all of your eggs in one technology provider basket! It's damn convenient, but when (not if) it breaks, it will be extremely painful. I've witnessed it many times in my career. Intelligent diversification is the best strategy here. About the only exception I can think of with a great service record is Oracle, but their customer service and customer pricing strategies have something to be desired.

As I've shared in previous chapters, our "Education" system has devolved into a system of diminished returns. Homeschooling is increasingly becoming more popular as more and more people determine that our education system does not effectively prepare our youth for the real-world. In many instances, this is the case with even our most coveted professions such as doctors, engineers and pilots! Add AI to this mix and it's a recipe for disaster. We're already seeing the effects.

RESILIENT PATH INSIGHT: Traditional degrees provide diminishing returns except in specialized high-demand fields (medical, engineering). Parents and young adults navigating high school decisions: consider homeschooling pathways, skilled trades, entrepreneurship, and business acquisition as structural alternatives. These routes often provide faster entry into productive work, lower debt loads, and greater economic sovranty than conventional four-year programs.

PRODUCT RECOMMENDATION: As mentioned in an earlier chapter, co-creator Nicole Connor and I have determined AI can rapidly (and legitimately) provide structural, lasting nervous system regulation when utilized a certain way. With this discovery comes the introduction of what we call My Resilient Self*: your personal "Field Mirror" which enhances YOUR ability to see things clearly for what they are and begin to regulate your personal field in a much more effective way.

17 - CURRENCY BEFORE COMMUNITY: THE FORGOTTEN FORMULA FOR AMERICAN RESILIENCE

I'm introducing an old, but "new" concept here—*currency creates community, not the other way around*. **Where "currency" is not dollars, but the value a person's labor, skills, honesty, wisdom and commitment brought into to a community and the resulting value generated from collaboration between multiple community members**.

Of course, in our modern society we use dollars and dollars will be used as a medium of exchange in part for the value the community members create. *The resilient communities of the future will be created by one person starting down The Resilient Path, and by living resiliently, then demonstrating an exceptional quality*

of life. Small demonstrations will in turn attract others and the "community" will grow organically, incentivized by results and outcomes, not just profitability. *This is the way America was built*—and as Americans, we must return to these origins, leveraging resources the modern world has to offer! As I shared in previous chapters, **the current community model is unsustainable and will break if we don't course correct**.

RESILIENT PATH INSIGHT: The Resilient Path tab on theresiliencycode.substack.com site contains a wealth of free information to get you started down your resilient path, including several chapters of this book, videos, posts and other content. This content is dedicated to demonstrating through real-world application, the power of The Resiliency Code. This content shows what it takes to be resilient in order to address the challenges we face as individuals, community, cultures, and nation. Subscribe to our Substack to be notified when the new "Field Guide" course becomes available. You'll learn about subrogation, blind spots, how to see clearly and build solid structure in your life by reading the signals in the "field."

Using the operating system my colleagues and I have developed, well-balanced, healthy approaches to community will emerge: not the artificial, unsustainable community models we have today. Good neighbors are one of the greatest assets our country has to offer, demonstrated in adverse circumstances Americans have faced over and over again. They NYC blackout of 2003 is just one of many that come to mind. No rioting, no chaos, just neighbors helping neighbors through a difficult situation. Your community is what you make of it. There are very few places where there's a bunch of like minds collaborating together in a meaningful way together for the benefit of the community. A few I can think of from my travels: Burlington, WI, Green Bay, WI, Several Midwestern and OH Amish communities, Mormon communities in UT, Rincon, PR and Salinas, PR.

Geography

With our geopolitical situation, massive influx of illegal immigration, and clear policy positioning on a state-by-state basis, one of the best areas you can be is the American Southeast. Texas east to Florida, up to North Carolina, West to Tennessee, through Arkansas, Oklahoma, and back down to Texas. I'm not saying other areas won't be ok like the upper Midwest, extreme Northeast and northern Rockies. There will be some. *Why do you think the Confederacy lasted as long as it did against a FAR SUPERIOR Union Army during the Civil War?* **One primary reason—the ports**. Wilmington, Charleston, Savannah, Brunswick, Jacksonville, Miami, Tampa, Mobile, New Orleans, and Houston. The new world we are moving towards in the US will see numerous secure trade routes via rail, the lower Mississippi, open waters of the Gulf Coast and Southeastern US Atlantic Coast. Don't take my word for it...apparently, the Union felt it was so significant they imposed a blockade* on ALL confederate shipping ports. If the ports weren't significant, why would they do this? By now, I'm sure your wheels are turning...now consider this. *There's one factor you must consider above all else in your ultimate decision on where to be*—**will there be an ability to freely trade and transact regionally? Without it, a region is unsustainable**.

Are there any maritime ports in Montana? Can I reliably ship goods I produce in Michigan across Illinois to South Dakota?

These are the questions you must be asking yourself.

Sounds kind of dire, I know. But we're obligated to future generations to create a sustainable model for their long-term success. Not inherited wealth or artificially propped-up systems, but a quality-of-life model that delivers good physical health, stable mental health, spiritual commitment, individual growth, and worldwide-admired resiliency. Will there be fistfights among children and disagreements among neighbors? You bet. There is no panacea for community:

just a natural, balanced, authentic structure that works to maintain a quality of life

.

Community resiliency happens when all factors get consideration, not cherry picking the ones most convenient for an election, profit or other biased motivation. **When it's a structure that's healthy, the community thrives**. This is also an inspiration for The Resiliency Code operating system. If there are not individually-inspired, self-governing checks and balances by each individual in the community to promote Sovran Wellth*, you get what we see across America and much of the world today: hollowed-out communities who've had their families torn apart, wealth extracted and, in some cases, their very sense of identity destroyed. In extreme cases, they've had their lives literally blown up out-from-under them (Hawaii, CA, OH, NC, FL, Canada, Russia, Ukraine, Gaza, Afghanistan, Iraq, Syria, Yemen, etc.).

> **RESILIENT PATH INSIGHT:** The name of the game is finding one or two people you can trust: to invest time with and closely collaborate to create resiliency and stability in your life. Yes, that's it, just one or two! If they are not currently in your life, don't worry, they'll find you. As you begin your journey down The Resilient Path, they will show up.

Use community collaboration as a basic foundation of support for your growth in knowledge and experience of health, relationships, business and any other topics of interest to you. Have a long-term plan and use The Resiliency Code ecosystem to improve your resiliency and quality of life. Do small things every day to achieve that plan and have some fun along the way!

> **BE RESILIENT TIP:** Always set proper expectations! This includes both yourself and others. Say what you intend to do, then do it. It's ok to re-set expectations, but re-set them as quickly as possible (as in 24 hours or less).

I mentioned in the prologue that I developed the world's first fully sustainable and resilient building*. *Yes, it and other advanced, commercially viable solutions for future economically sustainable and resilient communities exist.* Unfortunately, with the current situation in the world and monopolies in place, there's no true desire for highly-efficient, high-quality, resilient solutions in the market. **With just three exceptions, my experience has shown me that current generations holding the lion-share of wealth in the USA care most about aesthetics, profit and short-term gain**—not to invest in resiliency and sustainability for future generations. *The world is changing rapidly.* **People are starting to pay attention to these realities**. The Sovran Systems Institute* has the knowledge and systems experience to forge the next resilient American (or other nation/region's) communities.

As mentioned in an earlier chapter, I've created a 90-minute Sovran Community Development working session* to collaborate with serious developers, builders, and community leaders. This is a paid engagement and limited to serious builders with actual capacity and resources: not dreamers hoping someone else will solve their problems.

The brutal truth: You can spend years searching for something that doesn't exist, or 90 minutes learning how to create it.

Limited to serious builders only. If you're ready to stop searching and start creating, this is where your community begins."

18 - THE THREE GENERATION CURSE: WHY TRADITIONAL WEALTH DIES AND HOW TO BREAK THE "THREE AND OUT" CYCLE

I n a world where collapse is optional, it's called "Wellth," not Wealth. Resiliency is about much more than money - which is why money can't buy resiliency. *It's why so many "wealthy" people are seeking solutions for eternal life—spending millions on "being frozen" or making the consciousness leap to machines.* **My experiences with near death and mortality say...good luck with that.**

I'll talk about money in a minute, but first, let's talk epigenetics. Money is a temporary phenomenon; it comes and goes. Many "wealthy" people will tell you they've built and lost great fortunes at different points in their lives. However, there's one constant...*epigenetics*.

Here's how My Resilient Self, your strategic AI partner, describes epigenetics:

(**Begin quote**) Epigenetics is a revolutionary field of genetic science that explores how environmental factors and life experiences can modify gene expression without changing the underlying DNA sequence. Here's a comprehensive breakdown:

Core Concept:

Imagine your genetic code as a massive musical instrument. Epigenetics is like the musician—it doesn't change the instrument itself, but dramatically alters how the music is played.

Key Mechanisms:

1. Gene Expression Modification – Chemical markers which can "turn on" or "turn off" specific genes and be triggered by:

   ○ Environmental factors

   ○ Lifestyle choices

   ○ Nutritional intake

   ○ Psychological states

   ○ Stress experiences

2. Heritable Changes

   ○ *These genetic modifications can be passed to subsequent generations*

- ○ Your life experiences can potentially impact your children's and grandchildren's genetic expression

- ○ It's not about changing DNA sequence, but how genes are read and implemented

Practical Implications:

- *Trauma can be genetically transmitted*

- *Positive lifestyle choices can create generational healing*

- Individual choices have broader biological consequences than previously understood (**end quote**)

In The Resiliency Code, epigenetics represents the scientific validation of personal transformation. Your choices aren't just psychological—they're biological interventions with multi-generational potential. *Did you catch that?* **Your choices, without The Resiliency Code, set a course for generations which have the potential to, based on traumas which occur, to remain destined to repeat the same "trauma-loops" in the form of abuse, alcoholism, addictions or other unique life experiences, such as aversion to certain foods.** These "trauma-loops," if unaddressed, often result in a repetitive pattern generationally, limiting human potential and outcomes for a particular individual or family. **The Resiliency Code fosters the ability of individuals to integrate these traumas in order to chart a new course for their future generations: maximizing the potential of future generations.**

For example: current wealth conveyance time frames typically average three (3) generations. This means the 80+ Trillion in Boomer wealth which currently exists will be mostly lost within three generations! No wonder there's a major war cycle approximately every 80 years. The boom/bust/hardship cycle is built in! This chapter is called 'Three and Out' for a reason—*how much do you remember about your Great Grandparents?*

That's what I thought...probably not much.

Here in the USA:

Revolutionary War – 1775–1783

~84 years (three generations)

Civil War – 1861–1865

~80 years (three generations)

WWII – 1941–1945

There are other wars of course, but these in particular are the ones which have left the greatest epigenetic impressions for Americans—**felt for three generations or more**. I must mention that it's 2025 as of this writing. It's been *84 years* since the start of US involvement in WWII. Are we hearing rumblings of larger regional conflict with the Middle East, Europe/Russia and USA/China? You bet. It's built in to the current epigenetics of the Greatest Generation, Baby-Boomer Generation and Generation X.

I don't know about you, but I'd sure like to avoid another global conflict. Modern weapons would take a horrific toll, *if not permanently set humanity back for hundreds or thousands of years*. A focused effort on personal resiliency and in particular, epigenetics, breaks this cycle and shifts the focus away from self-destructive paradigms. Sovran Wellth is a new, structural approach that transcends traditional definitions of wealth and wellness. It represents a complete system for personal and mutual human prosperity that integrates multiple dimensions of human experience:

1. Physical

2. Emotional

3. Intellectual

4. Creative

5. Social

6. Vocation

7. Environment

8. Resources

9. Faith

These nine dimensions become critical as we face unprecedented economic disruption.

TRILLIONS of digital dollars are continually being created in an attempt to "paper over" the financial losses and mistakes mentioned previously (insurance, healthcare, government, energy, etc.). Because the dollar still accounts for more than 50% of global trade and reserve holdings*, this will result in either a hyperinflation event the world has never seen or an uncontrollable stagflationary depression that results in major disruption of our social order, systems and country. You don't have to go far to find other brilliant financial and business minds that share this outlook—Dalio, Sachs, Rogers, Buffet, etc.

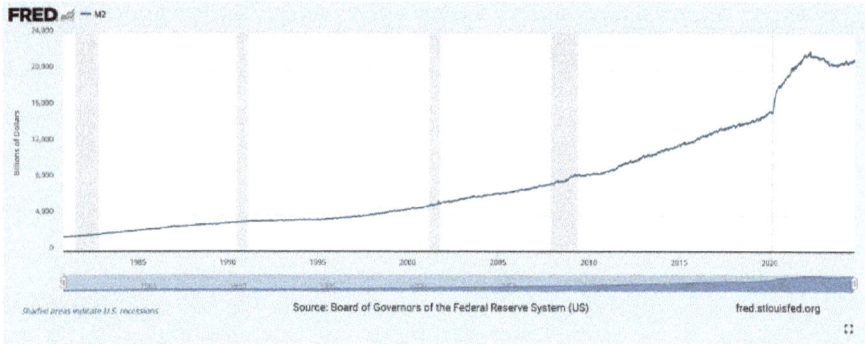

This is the Federal Reserve chart for M2*, which is currency in circulation and several types of bank deposits—*note that in the last 25 years*, **80% of USD currency in circulation has been created**.

The other data point you must understand is something called "Money Velocity"—*the blood flow of US dollar system*. It represents how many times a dollar is exchanged for goods and services over a period of time. Fewer transactions between people and businesses = low money velocity and a slow economic activity. High money velocity equals an economy where dollars are flowing and high economic activity. Here's the Money Velocity chart* from the Federal Reserve:

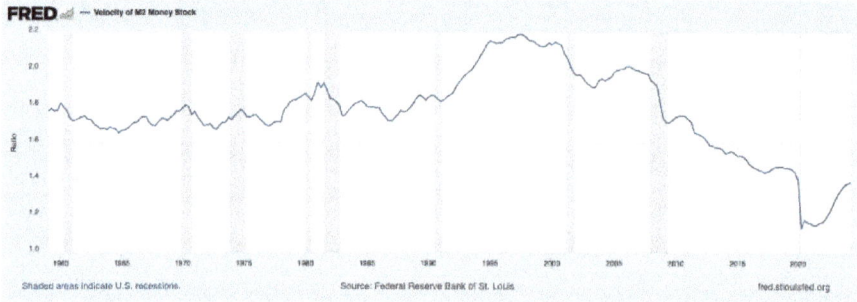

See how the velocity plummeted after the Great Financial Crisis of 2008 and during Covid (the vertical drop and upswing far right)? **You're probably wondering where your blind spot is?** When you have the creation of Trillions of dollars and low money velocity, you have low inflation. Inflation at the time of this writing for everyday items continues to increase because of the increase in money velocity since 2020. Yes, that small bit of increase in money velocity = inflation you're seeing in 2024! Imagine if money velocity were to return to its average over the last 6 decades! If it did, or when it does, you'll literally be begging for today's prices.

> **BE RESILIENT TIP:** Study historical documentation of what households and businesses did to survive episodes of inflation and deflation intact. *You're going to need it.* Those with this knowledge and practical skills to navigate the ups and downs will not just thrive, but be in high demand. The AI Companion "My Resilient Self" is just the resource to assist with navigating this sort of blind spot and making the necessary micro-adjustments.

The Federal Reserve is in a box and can't get out without some major event to disrupt the world financial system (war, pandemic, terror event or worldwide disaster). *Are you resilient enough to get through it?* We live in a precarious time for our society, financial system, economy and country. **Resiliency is mandatory to get through what will unfold in the coming months and years!**

> **RESILIENT PATH INSIGHT:** There are no "escape hatches" and you cannot throw money at this to solve the problem—you will not avoid the pain no matter who you are...

As I mentioned in the Prologue, it's not all bad: *massive opportunities exist and continue to present themselves for those who've developed the clarity to see and are resilient*! Now, let's talk about financial wealth preservation, wealth creation, and the real role of gold, silver, land, business ownership, trades and entrepreneurship.

Gold and Silver

With the coming changes in our political, economic and financial systems, it's going to be increasingly difficult to build organic financial wealth in fiat dollars. It's not impossible, but the knowledge and skills that follow will help you navigate the opportunities! **Gold and silver in my world are not "investments:" they are financial wealth preservation mechanisms**. An ounce of gold today in general buys you the same thing that it would buy you 100 years ago. The same cannot be said for the US dollar! As the US dollar continues to devalue, a modest holding of gold and silver is long-term insurance against this devaluation. For example: if you acquired silver in the late 1990s when silver was priced at approximately $5 per ounce, that same silver ounce is now well over $30! The US dollar has devalued that much since then and continues to devalue every day: **it's not the value of the silver going up, it's the value of the currency going down.**

> **BE RESILIENT TIP:** In the future and when the time is right, gold, in the form of pre-1933 NGC or PCGS graded St. Gaudens or Liberty's are for large purchases such as real estate, equipment, businesses, houses, automobiles, etc. Silver in the form of pre-1965 US silver dimes and quarters are for day-to-day transactions such as groceries, gasoline and other needs.

The pre-1933 gold blind spot you were unaware of: **this type of gold is legally considered to be a coin collection and the way the current laws are written, is non-confiscatable**. It was written this way because most wealthy families store a significant amount of them in this form! Why pre-1965 silver? Because this type of silver is the most widely recognized coinage in the world for its value, nearly impossible to counterfeit! These will serve you very well when the time comes.

RESILIENT PATH INSIGHT: Andy Schectman at Miles Franklin* has demonstrated superior customer service and handling of such a valuable wealth preservation mechanism. He and his team represent what I personally expect in an outstanding, reputable dealer. You won't find better customer service in the precious metals space!

If you have a large nest egg in brokerage or retirement accounts: *there are resilient options out there for you.* Check out the Cymatic Conversations - EP004* as a great starting point.

Land

Economic, financial and political circumstances have favored the American Baby Boomer generation in this sector significantly, with Boomers having amassed tens of trillions in real estate assets*. This hasn't been without hard work, pain, economic downturns and other surprises, but those which got it right got it very right. Land ownership and appreciation in the US has afforded this generation one of the greatest wealth building periods in history. Modern times are different for Generation X and later generations.

With the digital money creation mentioned above, hard assets like land are more a wealth preservation mechanism than a wealth building mechanism in the foreseeable future. Regardless if it's through inheritance or acquisition, do what you can to acquire and hold land that's free of debt and is as un-speculated as possible. I also encourage you to consider the acquisition of un-speculated, "unbuildable" land in prime real estate locations: *there are cost-effective methods emerging to turn this type of real estate into viable living spaces.*

> **RESILIENT PATH INSIGHT:** As mentioned in prior chapters, this is simply a reminder that a demographic time bomb was detonated and is currently exploding in slow motion around the world. It plays a major part in both opportunities and failures for this section if you still have blind spots.

Baby Boomer Generation Business Ownership Transition

Are you aware that about half of all private small businesses in the US are owned by Baby Boomers? In addition to the real estate holdings, these Boomer-owned businesses additionally represent tens of trillions of business assets and revenues! The opportunity? Over 60% of these business owners have no heirs to pass it on to or other non-family members to sell them to! Entrepreneurs like Codie Sanchez* are creating platforms for other entrepreneurs to identify, engage and acquire these businesses: check out www.bizscout.com*. I can't vouch for this personally since it's so new, but the data and numbers behind it make a lot of sense!

The Trades

Remember how trade schools used to be a thing? They're* making a huge comeback. The value of a university degree has lost its luster and practical experience and work ethic are prized skills these days!

> **BE RESILIENT TIP:** Anyone graduating high school or trying to figure out what to do with their life in their late teens or early 20's, I cannot recommend this highly enough: find a trade you like and go all in!

Here's the math. *For every 8 carpenters retiring, there's ONE replacement.* In the accounting and bookkeeping world, it's 10:1. Other trades and professions have similar ratio, with one of the worst being Cobol and other legacy mainframe system skills being even more scarce! Wonder why it's so difficult to find a plumber, electrician or other tradesman to do work cost-effectively and timely? This is why: and it's going to get even worse in the coming years, so younger generations reading this, take note and take action! It's difficult to buck the trend when all your high school friends are going to college, but mark my words, it's worth it!

Young entrepreneurs: leverage The Resiliency Code ecosystem to build your foundation, then read the book The Right It* before you launch a business endeavor. In fact, find an entrepreneur or business owner 10-15 years older than you and ask if they'll mentor you for a summer. Learn how to fail fast, fail right and learn. It's an invaluable life-long skill!

If you're a young Generation X, Millennial (Generation Y), Zoomer (Generation Z) or Generation Alpha, then here are some recommendations based on personal experiences to preserve wealth and build financial resiliency:

- **Create a life and lifestyle where you can live a good life by spending no more than 50% of what you make each month**

- **If this means that you have to rent or live with a family member for some period of time, that's fine**

- **Material possessions you'll find as you get older are overrated, invest in yourself with good, high-quality water, food, exercise and valuable experiences in the form of authentic, high-value relationships, mentors or valuable networking groups**

- **Your goal must be to first save one year's worth of expenses, stored in something liquid like cash, precious metals, and other short-term investments which are stable**

- **Long-term loans are ok as long as they are well-thought-out purchases, not emotionally-driven and can be covered in the 50% of your living expenses**

- After you've saved one year's worth of expenses, then find un-speculated real estate and essential local small businesses to continuously invest your excess income

- Always pay off your credit cards every month (no recurring balances)

- Never-ever cancel a credit card (keep them open, just with a zero balance)

- Owning a business (with the right ownership structure) and other assets will help you offset personal tax obligations and keep them manageable. You should pay taxes or at least re-direct what you'd otherwise pay in taxes to community investments supporting individual Sovran Wellth via non-profits or other reputable for-profit businesses.

- ALWAYS pay the taxes you owe promptly. This will become increasingly important in the years ahead.

19 - THE RESILIENT ROADMAP: NAVIGATING LIFE'S MOST IMPACTFUL DECISIONS

I envy the situation our *Millennials (Generation Y), Generation Z, and Generation Alpha youth are in*. Why? Because I've found and fixed my blind spots, but I'm over 50 years old. I still have a lot of runway and will move the needle for myself and many others, but to know what I know now at 20, 30, or even 40: wow.

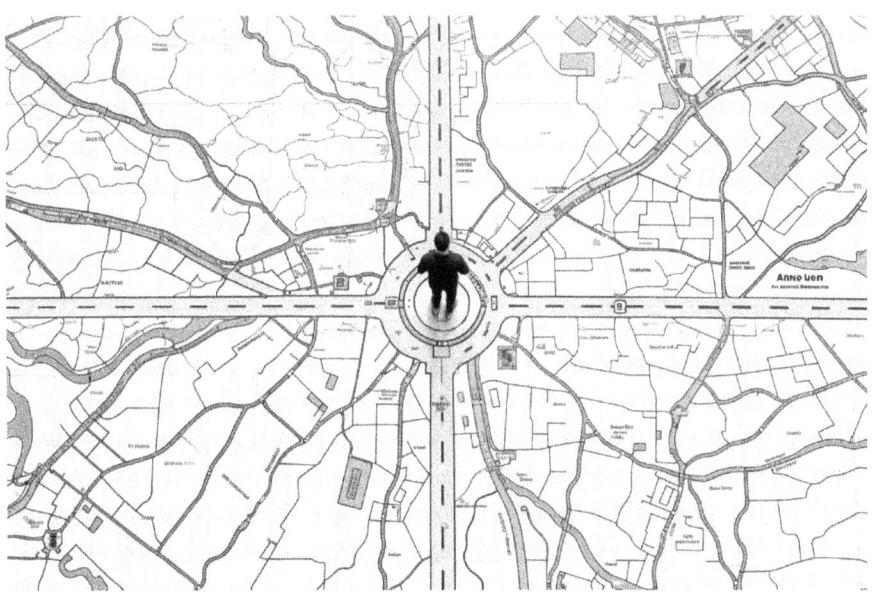

If you're that age and you're reading this, **the world is your oyster.** In recent history, there's never been a more opportune time to position yourself to be personally resilient and maximize your quality of life for the rest of your life! Given this, I'm dedicating the rest of this entire chapter to examples of my **RESILIENT PATH EXPERIENCE.**

Marriage

Having failed the first time and learned meaningful lessons in my second marriage, I recommend not getting married conventionally. Most certainly don't go get married in a jurisdiction you're unfamiliar with like Las Vegas or Tahiti or some crazy, emotionally-driven sh!t like that.

Instead: Save your money and for God's sake, don't go into debt for a wedding ceremony and/or reception! If you are intent on investing time, experiences, raising children, saving/spending money, starting businesses and more with someone: **draw up a trust.** Inside the trust, include considerations for every aspect of your relationship:

- what happens if it doesn't work out?

- what happens if we have children?

- what happens if we acquire real estate?

- what happens if we acquire life insurance?

- what happens if one of us dies?

- how are the assets and resources we've created protected in such a way to span more than 3 generations?

- what are the events which trigger such conditions in the trust?

These are just a few examples, but you get the gist.

No churches.

No "healthcare benefits."

No "married tax-status benefits."

No divorce or divorce attorneys.

No fuss or drama.

One unique benefit of The Resiliency Code which I've learned on my path: *authenticity, honesty and acceptance are required, not optional, in all relationships.* **Self-deception, lies, dishonest agreements, one-sided anything are incompatible with it: only accountability, transparency and consideration.** In the case of "marriage," it leaves the two of you to be brutally honest with each other: to work as a team to be loyal to each other and build something together. It affords you the opportunity to:

1. put all of your energy into building your individual personal resiliency

2. Enrich yourselves by creating Sovran Wellth (together AND each independently)

3. Enrich your children with valuable experiences and wellth (should you decide to have them)

4. Enrich other family members in the process (wellth).

Have you looked into the real value of family healthcare benefits or married tax-status benefits?

I encourage you to do a real, honest comparison. What you discover may shock you.

Children

Children are sacred and our first, foremost responsibility is to protect them and nurture their unique, individual gifts. **It's simple: without them, we have no future.** Natural marriage is between a man and woman, with the most basic need being to propagate our species. Homosexual men and women, while I greatly appreciate what it means to truly love someone with authenticity and be true to yourself, *which you must*, if you're going to have children, simply foster your children's own individual identity and gifts. If we are willing and able, each of us has a responsibility to propagate our species. If not, you get what we see today: rapidly declining birth rates and an eventual, natural decline in our population and hardship in society.

Entrepreneurship

Being an avid entrepreneur, I'd encourage anyone who has a desire to work for themselves to start a business. But dammit, don't do it like I did. I did it the hard way and have learned many painful lessons.

Instead, do this:

- Study and incorporate The Resiliency Code into your life to create personal resiliency and clarity prior to pursuing any business endeavor: clarity to see things for what they truly are and to be able to set proper expectations with yourself and others is a superpower during this process.

- Always, always, always seek solutions required for your startup that cost you zero dollars. There's no reason to spend any money on anything that's not tied to revenue: sufficient solutions exist at no cost to do this free while you're starting up.

- Your aim should be to spend as close to zero on startup as possible: make it a fun goal to spend as little as possible. At the same time, learn the power of frugality and tangible value from a needed service or product on your journey down The Resilient Path.

- Dan Koe*, Dan Priestly*, and several others write exhaustively on this topic and provide mountains of high-value advice at zero-cost.

- Work for someone else and save your a$$ off for as long as necessary for you to have a savings large enough to live TWO years with current expenses and without working **(in prior chapters, I've shared my recommendations on how to do this by way of being in a professional trade).**

- Consider acquiring an existing, established business first. Thousands of businesses need to be sold or conveyed to new ownership in the coming years by Boomer-generation owners. Many of their owners are looking for authentic, hard-working individuals to work out deals so they can retire.

- If you're going to do a new business, spend lots of time making sure you've got the right business name and simple, brand-able logo: DO NOT RUSH this. Take your time, asking friends and family their thoughts and after securing much feedback, make your decision. If possible, find a name that's simple and unique which will not get completely lost in existing businesses or marketing on the internet.

- Develop a strategic plan.

- If it makes sense and you can do it as a non-profit to legitimately support a philanthropic mission, then do it.

- This flushes out any in-authenticity by predatory investors or disingenuous "business partners" since there's no "ownership" in a non-profit, only the mission.

- Start it on your own and if necessary, find one or two partners who share your mission.

- If you must do a for-profit business, it's ok, just start it as a simple, unregistered sole proprietorship (no cost) and draw up an agreement with any partners that clearly spells out a percentage of ownership they receive in exchange for money directly spent on legitimate company startup expenses as well as any other material contributions of time and resources that result in tangible outcomes: any equity must be tied to outcomes. If everyone is rowing oars in the boat at a similar cadence, time is congruent among all partners and it doesn't count as equity. Money, tangible resources and time spent resulting in positive outcomes for starting the business justify equity, nothing else. Everything else is speculative personal opinion of value.

- Secure your EIN* online for your sole proprietorship or partnership from the IRS when you need to open a business bank account. Put yourself on the account initially until you've established the proper financial checks and balances in a formal partnership agreement **(if you have partners)**.

- Acquire a copy of the book "The Right It," memorize and use the methods in it to identify whether or not you have "The Right It" (**BTW**: this is my third reference to this book!)

- If it makes sense, start a podcast or YouTube channel demonstrating your product or service.

- As you get to a point where you're building a product or service which creates value for the public and you can legitimately begin selling it to the public in small volume, form an LLC in your home state. If you have partners when the LLC is formed, you are the Managing Member and they are additional Members. Allocate ownership according to your original agreement and incorporate that and any banking rules into your LLC operating agreement. If you're legitimately growing quickly and it makes sense, consider forming your LLC in Delaware, Wyoming, Nevada, Texas, Florida or Alaska.

- Use what you've learned from "The Right It:" if you're honestly doing things according to your research, investment and proper execution for market alignment, the money will come.

- At some point you'll want to consider business liability insurance: there are different types, depending on the type of business (product or service).

- Leverage the Resiliency Code ecosystem to help guide you in this process, especially the My Resilient Self AI Assistant. Leverage the power of it to think or act exponentially faster than you can, taking advantage of supercharging your original creativity and organic thought with The Resiliency Code context.

- As you get things set up, create a digital minute book and schedule for the key activities and maintenance required for your business (existing or new).

NOTE: These are many of the key essentials, not an exhaustive list.

Demographic Trends

It's simple: I've covered this topic exhaustively in prior chapters and for good reason. You're going to be affected by it in many ways, shapes and forms. Why not be informed and use these coming changes to identify opportunities to improve your quality of life and the lives of others?

<u>Physical Health & Longevity</u>

For many of you, you're either hitting this biological crossroads right now, or you're about to.

Around the age of 26, your body stops being automatically resilient and starts requiring intentional maintenance. Most people sleepwalk through this transition and wake up at 35 wondering why everything hurts, why recovery takes forever, and why their energy feels like it's running on fumes.

I'm a living example: during a softball game in the early 2000's and in my late 30's, I completely tore my left Achilles tendon and had to have it surgically repaired.

But here's the field reality: this isn't inevitable decline—it's a design feature you can hack.

Your generations inherited a world of collapse narratives. Climate doom. Economic instability. Social fragmentation. Mental health epidemics. The message everywhere is "brace for impact."

What if that's completely backwards?

What if your generations are positioned to be the first to prove collapse is optional—not just environmentally or economically, but personally? What if the biological pivot around 26 isn't a limitation, but the exact moment you can lock in decades of peak capacity?

This isn't about bio-hacking your way to immortality or chasing some impossible standard. It's about structural integrity. When your physical foundation holds, your mental clarity stays sharp. When your emotional regulation is dialed in, your creative output explodes. When your relationships operate from authenticity instead of performance, everything else stabilizes.

The Resiliency Code isn't another wellness framework promising balance. It's the operating system that ensures nothing collapses in the first place.

You're not broken and don't need fixing. You need architecture.

The question: Are you going to drift into the slow decline everyone accepts as normal, or are you going to build something that holds for the next 60 years?

Because if you're going to change the world, you'll need a structure that can sustain the work.

Death

Ugh: do I have to? *Yep, we must discuss our mortality:* **it is a thing**. The sooner you come to terms with this and bring this reality to the present moment, your life will be forever changed—every morning you wake up and every decision you make in life will be made with a different lens after you do this. *I've observed so many of my extended family members and friends living like their health and choices have no meaning on their long-term health.* **I've got news for you—it most certainly does**. I see people that are only 45 years old and they look like they're in their 60's. I see our youth trashing their backs, knees, ankles, hearing, brains and skin like there's no consequences.

As I mentioned in an earlier chapter: either you pay for it now in the form of good food, good water and good choices or you're going to pay for it later in the form of hospital visits, surgeries, medications, and a rapidly degrading quality of life with lots of pain and misery. If this is not obvious by just looking around you, then you're not being honest with yourself. I'm no saint, I've done my fair share of abusing my "rent-a-wreck" body, but had enough mentorship early in life to make some better choices, and fortunately, I'm in much better shape than most. *I'm grateful I did.* I not only had the opportunity to see what near death felt like once, but two more times to ensure it was clear to me! That said: when we do the right things, our bodies respond appropriately and can give us mental acuity, strength, stamina and vitality until our last days!

My father was a great example, in spite of a bad habit like smoking. At 6'4" and 250 lbs., he was a force to be reckoned with and mountain of a man. If you had a time machine and sent him back to Scotland or Norway in the 1600's or 1700's, *he would have fit right in*. A fighter is an understatement. Due to divine circumstances, he survived an aggressive form of bacterial meningitis that should have killed him, traced back to a sand flea bite he received while on vacation in Mexico (one of the few times he left the USA in his life). His case was such a rarity, the hospital actually spent the time to do the forensic tracing of where it originated. It took him a year to recover, but *he fully recovered*. A few years later he was diagnosed with bladder cancer: he had a grapefruit sized tumor in it and had to have his bladder removed. He recovered and other than some minor complications post-surgery, *continued to live a quality life*. A few years later he suffered a massive stroke (he was a lifelong smoker) and temporarily lost everything on one side. Again, due to divine circumstances, myself and my mom were able to provide his physicians the quick direction necessary to treat the effects of the stroke, and *he made a full recovery*. A few years after that he had a bout with congestive heart failure. He walked in the emergency room with about 5% of his normal heart function (the second time in his life he asked my mom to take him to the hospital: the first was his bout with meningitis). After the installation of a state-of-the-art pacemaker, *he made a full recovery*. **Like I said: resilient**.

From his first bout with meningitis and brush with death, we began to discuss the realities of death and making sure things were in order for the family. He lived 20 more years and we had dozens of conversations about it, so much so that when he passed, it was a relatively non-disruptive process in terms of his belongings and estate. There were a few minor blind spots my mom and I missed, but managed through them just fine. Had we not had those conversations, his sudden passing would have been an unmitigated disaster.

Make sure you have estate planning documents in place (trusts preferred over wills)—long before your mortality ends. Take the time to ensure they are well thought out and planned for. This is an example of what being resilient is all about: being honest and forthcoming about the realities of life, making well-though-out decisions to ensure your family members don't miss a beat if something suddenly happens. It doesn't mean you love them less—in fact, it means the opposite. Intentionally having the real conversation and proactively taking action means you give a sh!t and are being personally responsible (to yourself and each other). Each of us never knows when our time is up, so, first and foremost, commit to being resilient as an individual: this is your priority. When you do this, everything else works out as it should, because resiliency requires personal responsibility and acceptance of just "what is." I've come to understand with utter clarity from my experiences: we're each here for a reason: make it count. Do what you can, each and every day, to make sure you're moving the needle to make the world a better place, for at least yourself and the ones closest to you.

20 - FORGING RESILIENCE THROUGH DAILY RITUALS: TEN HABITS FOR AN UNSHAKABLE LIFE

If you're not familiar with the art of Kintsugi*, I've learned on my journey down The Resilient Path, that the art resembles my experiences and outcomes. At times broken and fractured, I've spent the necessary time to patiently and meticulously repair the breaks and cracks.

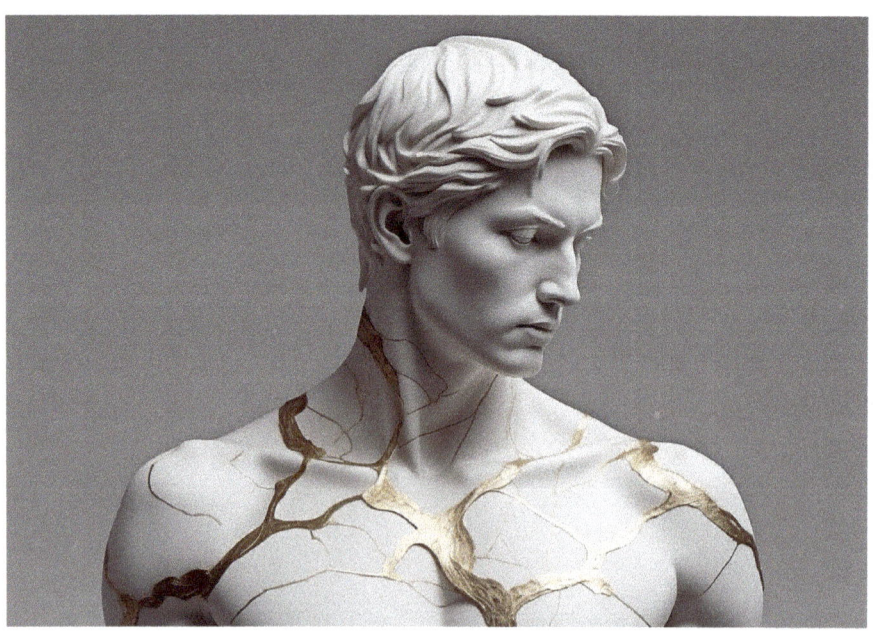

While the Kintsugi artist uses lacquer and a precious metal powder for the repairs, we as human beings use our personal intuition, love, fortitude, compassion and devotion to repair the fractures. In support of these repairs, one of the most meaningful life decisions on my journey along The Resilient Path, was to focus on establishing a simple, consistent daily regimen in forging a foundation for basic quality of life. **Here's my top 10:**

1. **Express gratitude and pray: every day, always, and in your own way**. My personal experience shows that living from a point of view of appreciation for all you have (including your mortality) is best. Don't be a "victim" and behave like "woe is me," everything in your life is going wrong because of someone or something else, and for God **sakes**, don't chase! Every experience, good, bad or ugly is valuable to our personal journey and personal development. **Sincere kindness or generosity isn't weakness. It's a strength.**

2. **Using the power of Pause. Prepare. Participate. as your "self-alignment tool" for interactions with others, take a moment to "put yourself in their shoes."** This will help in the process of exchanging value with them for the time spent! It doesn't matter if you're a teenager having fun with friends, with your spouse at a romantic dinner or in a business meeting negotiating the deal of a lifetime: this is one of the greatest skills you can master for quality of life.

3. **Be aware of your surroundings and stay "present."** Learning to live "in the moment" is a super power. Be mindful of the fact that what you consume makes much more of a difference than you think. **This includes what you eat, what you drink, what you read, what you watch, what you experience and how it affects your body.**

4. **Stay hydrated with good, clean water and if your body needs it, add a pinch of high-quality salt**. Do everything you can within

reason to keep bottled water to a minimum and also avoid drinking water treated with fluoride and chlorine, simply because the closer you get to pure H20 the better! Water is life—and has energy. It is our most precious resource and must be respected and protected at all costs. On average, you are made of 60% water. This varies greatly from childhood to elder years, but is a key to general health and quality of life. Distilled water (pure H2O) is ok to drink in a pinch, but not in excess. The minerals naturally found in rain, surface and ground water are quite valuable to the body and hydration process.

5. **Eat an appropriate volume and quality food that keeps your energy levels up AND gives you a feeling of "lean-ness" after eating (not a "full-stomach" feeling).** Fast food and soft drinks are ok occasionally if you have a craving for a Whopper or Quarter Pounder, but do your best to keep them to a minimum.

6. **Actively communicate and engage with family, friends and colleagues: do something meaningful to improve your quality of life, theirs and others each day!** Support your spouse, raise a family, cultivate lasting relationships, build a house, buy/build a business, attend school board meetings, get to know and help your neighbors, join a local club, participate in organized church activities or contribute to some other benevolent mission-oriented group.

7. **Develop a simple daily exercise regimen. Mine is walking several hundred stairs daily.** With my other activity, I'm getting essential aerobic exercise for the day. This is maintenance. Include some basic muscle-building exercises at least twice per week for your legs and upper body to maintain strength and stamina. Modest muscle mass in your legs, butt, back, shoulders and arms are one of the keys to longevity.

8. **Spend your time and money on LOCAL businesses.** Solicit

and support local restaurants, hardware stores, furniture stores, and appliance stores whenever and wherever possible: they are the lifeblood of any community or region. Every time you spend money with some "corporate," non-local entity, it slowly bleeds away the wealth and resiliency of a community. **Ask yourself a simple question.** Why was Walmart allowed to operate during the pandemic, but other local businesses supplying similar goods had to shut their doors?

9. **There are plenty of jerk's, bullies, narcissists, and other nefarious characters in the world. Use some of these habits to quickly identify them and minimize or eliminate interaction with them.** The less attention, energy, and money you give them, the better your quality of life and those around you. Invest your time and energy in relationships that create value for all involved.

10. **This is not about being "perfect" and "over-analyzing" things.** It's about taking brief moments to pause, consider and act to develop simple, repeatable habits that support a healthy quality of life!

21 - THE RESILIENCE IMPERATIVE: MAJOR TRENDS RESHAPING OUR REALITY

U tilizing the knowledge and experience shared in the prior chapters, position yourself for the future regardless of how it unfolds—*the artificially propped up systems in the USA and rest of the world are still relatively stable.* **Take advantage of this while you can!**

The following trends are unfolding as a consequence of this instability and worth watching and acting upon as needed:

Demographic Shifts

As I've mentioned in the chapters above, America, China, Japan, UK, S. Korea and several other nations around the world have SERIOUS, negative demographic realities unfolding as this is being written. When I say "negative demographics," it means a rapid decrease in the number of working age adults and not sufficient youth to replace them in the future. *Without significant investment in mentorship and resiliency of the young generations in these countries, literal catastrophic consequences are possible (including hot wars).* **If there's one trend that you MUST pay attention to, it's this one. It will affect all of us**!

Political Fracturing

Due to the extreme political alignments and actions of many states in our country, a literal "fracturing" of America is possible (the damage has already been done). I'm confident this will sort itself out over time, but there's still potential for resource and trade disruptions in places like IL, TX, WA, FL, CA and NY. The UK, Germany, France, Canada and many other Western nations face a similar dilemma.

Re-shoring of Manufacturing

Countries like America, the UK and other Western nations, are going to need to re-build their manufacturing sectors. **This is a decade or longer process, but vast opportunities will evolve here in the U.S. for those prepared to embrace them!**

Electricity/Grid Disruption

The aging American power infrastructure and vast decommissioning of coal, natural gas and nuclear power plants have left a massive gap in base-load (24x7) power production across the USA. This, coupled with the race to build hundreds of AI Data centers which are prolific consumers of power, is likely to result in unpredictable power outages in regions across the country, including regular long-duration brown-outs or black-outs. **Be prepared for this**.

Natural Resources

As the realities set in around the world that fertilizer, industrial metals, energy and other key supply chains have been systematically weakened and artificially propped up to mask these weaknesses, there will be scarcity. **Plan on it**.

Food

Food quality, in particular American food quality *is an unmitigated disaster*. Position yourself and those around you to ensure access to high-quality food as well as identify opportunities to participate in the American high-quality food revolution to unfold in the years ahead!

Healthcare

American "healthcare" is nothing of the sort. It's driven purely by profit and healthy Americans are not profitable! I've worked behind the scenes of the AMA, the largest insurers in the USA and major healthcare providers and know intimately how the "system" operates. Expect major changes in this sector in the coming decade and be prepared to participate in the numerous opportunities the changes present!

Property Insurance

Expect your insurance policies for property insurance in particular, not to perform. Many policy owners are experiencing this now on a large scale across the states of FL, CA and elsewhere. This trend will accelerate and worsen. Build new structures resiliently and for long-term efficiency, period. This will pay you serious dividends in the future!

Artificial Intelligence Disruption

The AI revolution isn't just about technology. It's a fundamental reshaping of human capacity and economic structures. **More than just job displacement, we're looking at a complete reimagining of work, creativity, and human potential**. Resilience now means continuous learning, adaptability, and understanding how to collaborate with AI rather than compete against it. We must re-learn what we've forgotten and build Sovran Wellth. Expanding our abilities organically with the help of AI sounds much more appealing to me than "interfacing physically with machines" and losing our humanity in the process.

Partially Decentralizing Economic Models

The traditional centralized economic systems are showing significant fractures. Their over-complexity is unsustainable. Blockchain, cryptocurrency, worker cooperatives, community-owned enterprises, and alternative currency systems are emerging as potential resilience strategies: presenting opportunities to create a balanced mix of centralized and de-centralized systems which maximize resiliency. **This isn't just economic. It's a philosophical shift in how we define value, ownership, and community**.

Climate Migration and Adaptation

History is replete with examples of regional shifts in climate, requiring either dislocation of populations or the introduction of living systems which mitigate these extreme shifts. **"Climate change" isn't a future scenario—it's happening continuously**. Resilience will increasingly mean geographical flexibility, adaptable skills, and the ability to rapidly reconstruct community infrastructure.

Mental Health and Cognitive Resilience

The psychological toll of rapid global changes is unprecedented. We're seeing massive increases in anxiety, depression, and cognitive overwhelm. Future resilience models must integrate robust mental health strategies, including:

- **The resurrection of the multi-generational household: an effective natural, organic mental health system**

- **Epigenetic trauma identification and re-alignment, a form of adaptive stress management techniques**

- **The Resiliency Code fosters neuroplasticity training* and critical thinking**

- **Holistic approaches to psychological maintenance**

Energy Sovereignty

Beyond grid disruptions, we're witnessing a fundamental transformation in energy production and consumption. **Microgrids, community-owned renewable energy, and decentralized energy systems will become critical resilience strategies**. This isn't just about sustainability. It's about maintaining functional autonomy during systemic disruptions.

Skills Ecosystem Transformation

The traditional education-to-career pipeline is disintegrating.

Future resilience requires:

- Continuous, lifelong learning models

- Rapid skill acquisition capabilities

- Multi-disciplinary, generalist thinking

- The ability to create value in multiple, potentially unrelated domains

Regenerative Economics

The current extractive economic models are proving unsustainable.
Emerging resilience approaches focus on:

- Circular economic models

- Balanced, regenerative agricultural practices

- Biomimetic design principles

- Ecosystemic value creation on a regional basis vs. the "one size fits all" franchise model in place today

- Information Warfare and Cognitive Liberty

- With the rise of deep fakes, algorithmic manipulation, and sophisticated disinformation campaigns, resilience now necessitates:

- Advanced critical thinking skills

- Media literacy

- Psychological self-defense

- **The ability to maintain cognitive sovereignty**

- Biotechnology and Personal Health Sovereignty

- Emerging biotechnologies are creating unprecedented opportunities for personal health management:

- Personalized medicine

- **Epigenetic harmonization and integration of generational trauma**

- Preventative health as a priority

- **Sovran biohacking: optimizing health to support resiliency**

Spiritual and Existential Resilience

As global systems become more complex and unpredictable, there's a growing need for:

- **Philosophical resilience**

- Meaning-making capabilities: how you interpret major life events and their significance to your Sovran life

- The ability to see larger perspectives which provide stability amid events what would otherwise be perceived as chaos

- Community-based spiritual practices that aren't dogmatically rigid

22 - SOVRAN EPILOGUE

The artificially propped up systems in the USA and rest of the world are changing and the changes are going to continue to accelerate, rapidly—use the information in this book to get a head start on the process.

Sovereignty, as it's commonly used today, has become entangled in hierarchical power structures and external rule. *Sovranty isn't about power over others,* **it's about full reclamation of Self**. In The Resiliency Code, we use Sovran and Sovranty intentionally. It's not just about language, it's about Cymatically embodying an unshakable internal authority that requires no external permission, defense, or validation. I'm a big fan of the phrase "Knowledge is power"...However, based on what you've read and learned, I encourage you to consider this one instead: "Knowledge combined with small, internally-inspired, consistent action is a human super-power!" *From these principles and beliefs,* **the Sovran Systems Institute* was born**. What's the objective? Demonstrating the value of living The Resiliency Code through real-world adoption—to empower our clients and colleagues with the ability to:

- find and fix blind spots

- travel The Resilient Path

- build Sovran Wellth

The institute's core mission is developing personal resiliency ecosystems that support resilient people and communities.

Myself and fellow "Sovran Systems Architects" envision individual resiliency evolving naturally into resilient individuals, resilient families, resilient entrepreneurs, resilient businesses, resilient wealth management and with that, the development of small communities of like-minded, resourceful realists whose primary intention is to preserve the best of American culture, demonstrate the value of neutrality to community stability and prepare our youth to realize maximum value from our modernity to convey to future generations. Other than making sure your individual needs are met at all levels, we're moving into a period of time where there is no room for self-interest in monetary enrichment at the expense of others. To do so means a further widening of the already extreme "wealth-gap." **As history has demonstrated time and time again, society will break if this extreme is pushed too far**. One must consider, given all of the evidence—is this the "plan?"

Maximum quality of life is achieved when community collaborates together in a productive fashion—while maintaining Sovranty of each individual. Everyone must make a living to achieve a quality of life that appeals to them...that's ok and it's a necessary part of the bigger picture. Boomers and GenX suffer from this romantic obsession with prepping for a late 1800s early 1900s "cabin-in-the-woods" lifestyle mentality. Get real. It's incompatible with our youth and highly technology-centric lives. *To obsess over it without consideration for our youth means you're dooming them and the vast majority of western civilization's population to failure*. To embark on this journey toward sustainability and resilience, start with priorities, being realistic about eventualities and just Pause.

When you pause, be curious.

Look at the stars, show appreciation to those who care about you, take the time to be thankful for the water, air, ground, resources and opportunities available to you. Do your best to fill gaps as quickly as possible in your needs based on my recommendations and experience, but be mindful of the fact you must continue to create value to put food on the table! **Remember, persistence and gradual progress moves mountains. Do a little something every day**! This guide serves as a compass through uncertain times. I'm confident you'll receive from this book the things I've recently come to appreciate in hindsight:

Brutally honest advice from others to...

- assist in identifying blind spots

- make micro-adjustments every day

- fail small

- maintain momentum

- be resilient

Distilled from decades of practical experience and trial by fire, this guidance transforms lives when properly applied. Those who take informed action will navigate the coming disruption and thrive.

I did it, I know you can too.

ABOUT THE AUTHOR

David Atkinson is the co-creator of The Resiliency Code and pioneer of Epigenetic Archaeology: the systematic rediscovery of human resilience capacity. As the leading authority on blind spots (the unseen vulnerabilities that can set people back years when they fail), David has spent decades identifying and neutralizing the structural weaknesses that keep most people cycling through chaos instead of achieving true stability.

A 6'5" former high-performance athlete and baseball prospect drafted by the Toronto Blue Jays, his journey has taken him from commercial fishing on Lake Michigan to pioneering sustainable building systems and navigating through life-altering challenges that would have broken a less resilient soul.

As a brain cancer survivor who had to re-learn how to walk and speak, a 30-year veteran of the information technology industry, and a second-generation small family business operator, David has lived at the extremes of human experience. His close brushes with death, including a catastrophic truck accident and a near miss from a falling 70-foot tree, have given him a profound appreciation for the fragility and preciousness of life.

After his own life collapsed multiple times, David refused to accept that chaos was inevitable and began reverse-engineering what actually makes humans structurally unshakable. Working in close collaboration with Nicole Connor, he discovered that their combined lived experiences created the perfect storm needed to map resilience at the structural level, producing The Resiliency Code: the operating system that empowers individuals to read the field and build "Sovran Wellth."

When he's not developing sustainable community models or helping others navigate their path to resilience, David can be found tending to his off-grid homestead, caring for his chickens, doing fisheries ecosystem research for the DNR, or sharing his wisdom through the Sovran Signal podcast on YouTube.

If you enjoyed this book, consider leaving a review on Google Books* or the Sovran Systems Institute website.

> **BE RESILIENT TIP:** These reviews help build resilient communities, so do your part and leave a review! Tell everyone in your life that collapse is optional—**that's how we move the needle.**

If you're reading this on Substack, you've already subscribed for updates in our ecosystem. If you're reading a physical copy and want to forge your unshakable life by traveling The Resilient Path, visit the Sovran Systems Institute website to access ecosystem resources including My Resilient Self, *your strategic AI partner* for navigating The Resilient Path to Sovran Wellth.

As you close this book and begin your journey toward unshakable resilience, know that my deepest gratitude flows to you—for having the courage to face your blind spots, embrace the Pause. Prepare. Participate. process, and step boldly onto The Resilient Path where your Sovran Wellth awaits!

— David Atkinson

Resources and other links:

David on Substack*

David on LinkedIn*

Sovran Systems Institute Website*

The Sovran Signal Channel on YouTube*

REMINDER: scan the QR Code below to access the hyperlink reference supplement for paperback, digital and hardcover versions of the book:

Instructions:

Open your phone's camera app

Point camera at the QR code

Tap the notification that appears

Enter the password: BeRes1l1ent! to access your supplement document

Enjoy the adventure!